CW01432033

Even while they sleep

PETER WARING

Trigger Warning: This book contains sensitive discussions of death, detailed descriptions of funerals, and aspects of funeral preparation.

Disclaimer: This is a work of nonfiction based on the personal experiences of the author as a funeral director. In order to protect the privacy of individuals, some names, identifying details, and circumstances have been changed.

Published by Softwood Books
Office 2, Wharfside House, Prentice Road, Stowmarket, Suffolk, IP14 1RD

Paperback ISBN: 978-0-9526197-2-7
Hardback ISBN: 978-0-9526197-3-4
First edition November 2024

CONTENTS

CONTENTS

1.
IN THE BEGINNING

The title of this book came to me a number of years ago when I first thought of writing a memoir of my life as a Funeral Director. A profession I had, for much of my life, never known anything about or even considered doing.

'Can't you just do an ordinary job?' my daughter, Diane, asked me when I first announced I was to become a funeral director. My previous occupation was working in a factory making artificial teeth - a non-topic of conversation if ever there was one. And now, Death! Perhaps one can understand the look of horror from my children.

Let's first clarify my role in the 'tooth factory.' It was an American owned company set up in Brighton in 1938. We made around 30 million artificial teeth a year, employing 300 staff. I always had to explain we did not make dentures but the teeth themselves, which a dental technician would put on the denture. Early in my career at Dentsply an elderly cleaner at the local primary school asked me what I did. When I told her I made artificial teeth, she immediately took out her dentures to show me the problem she was having with her denture.

"No," I said, "I just make the teeth."

A lesson in being more careful in my explanation of the work I did.

Originally, the company made teeth only in porcelain, requiring a number of fine hand skills for creating the blends and fixings using gold-clad pins and palladium coils; valuable precious metals. Florescence was also added to the porcelain powders, otherwise the teeth would look like tombstones under artificial light. Working conditions were hot but immaculately clean as you could not sell teeth containing little black specks. In the 1950s, my father made the first plastic teeth using acrylic materials. He realised that you could mould a variety of items in plastic and made some nuts and bolts in plastic. The management said plastic to make such items would never catch on, so refused to allow any further development. A huge lost opportunity in hindsight. In the late 1980s the production of porcelain teeth ceased.

I initially worked in production. This role covered powder mixing for the different ranges of colours in each range of teeth, moulding, stoving, trimming, necking, coning, drilling, undercutting, carding, and quality control. These were all different techniques and procedures in which staff had to be trained, and manual dexterity was a vital skill required for many of these. With the introduction of equal opportunities legislation, it remained a huge challenge to find men willing, or able, to spend time doing fiddly repetitive jobs. But with the introduction of employment legislation my role changed to become Personnel Manager, and I think it was that experience of interviewing and dealing with staff concerns that enabled me to cope later with the bereaved and their emotions, grief and sometimes anger.

In the last two years with the company, I also covered as Production Manager. One of the first jobs asked of me was to make 30 people redundant because of lack of orders. A horrible and difficult job. Three months later we had an order for one and a half million teeth from Kenya and I needed to employ thirty staff. And, of course, they all needed training. I was reasonably successful at the role, I think, but found it really challenging trying to meet daily production targets whilst always striving to lower production costs. However, I received far less job satisfaction than before I was promoted. Each day started with zero and then go, go, go to reach your target that day. With the investment they made in new technology, it required me to set up twenty-four-hour shifts. The evening shift was not a problem to man, but the night shift was a nightmare. Defect rates rocketed, and it was my job to try to overcome the problems. To reduce costs, the American owners dictated that all staff would be responsible for their own quality control, and I was responsible for making this happen. However, I knew it would never work. This got me into trouble, but three months later the American company had a 100 percent recall because of quality defects. I had none.

What led me to change my job, then? My grandfather was the sales director of the distribution company which sold dental equipment as well as the teeth we made, travelling throughout the world. My father had worked at Dentsply all his working life. My prospects there looked good - even the possibility of becoming the managing director, like my father. However, the pressures to ever increase efficiency and reduce costs, without having full control of procedures, was taxing.

At the time, I thought nothing of it. I had a secure job and I was not looking to change my career. My wife and I attended a funeral at Jarvis Brook, near Crowborough. Something in the manner of the funeral director directing the funeral appealed to me. He was smart, well organised, and conducted the funeral in a discrete, controlled manner. It was as good of a 'good send-off' as you could hope for.

It was only some months later that I saw an advertisement in an old Evening Argus newspaper for a funeral director and I thought 'that's the sort of job I would like.' The newspaper was already a week old. In fact, I was just about to light the coal fired Rayburn with it, but I showed it to my wife, and we agreed we should pray about it. We had been reading our devotional for that day and found ourselves reading to the end of Joshua, chapter 24. It reads:

'Now fear the Lord and serve him with all faithfulness. Throw away the gods your forefathers worshipped beyond the river and in Egypt, and serve the Lord. But if serving the Lord seems undesirable to you, then choose for yourselves this day whom you will serve, whether the gods your forefathers served beyond the river or the gods of the Amorites in whose land you are living. But as for me and my household, we will serve the Lord.'

My father and grandfather had worked in the dental company all their lives. And 'Choose today,' the passage said. The advert was already a week old, so an immediate response was indicated. And 'as for me and household'; when I phoned up, I was told to bring my wife along to the interview as it was very much a family commitment! At Dentsply I was now under pressure to make Sunday an ordinary workday. In the funeral business I knew, as a funeral director, I would have to work occasionally on a Sunday, but I would be serving people, not trying to achieve ever higher manufacturing targets. So, I phoned to ask if the vacancy was still open and expressed my interest.

At the interview, I was told I would be on call twenty-four hours a day for three weeks in every four. This was in the days before mobile phones, so someone had to be at home in order to answer the phone outside office hours, hence the request to bring my wife along to the interview. A family commitment? That was to prove very true, even involving the children.

So, out of the blue, I changed jobs. After twenty years with Dentsply I had now found a vocation which was to give me huge satisfaction for the next thirty years. Little did I realise what a wide range of new skills I would need to learn. It involved arranging and conducting funerals, of course, but also how to deal with the deceased, the legislation and documentation required, coffin making, engraving, knowing the signs of and tests for death, embalming, even learning how to remove a ring from a finger without damaging the skin. I had to deal with nursing homes, hospitals, hospices, doctors, vicars, registrars, gravediggers, cemeteries, and graveyards - yes there is a difference - florists, memorial masons, newspapers, printers, solicitors, the police, the coroner. Then, where to hire additional hearses, limousines, horse-drawn carriages, and hire casual bearers. Any one or more of these could be necessary to be called upon immediately for any funeral arrangement. There was correspondence to confirm details to all involved, unbelievably before the age of the internet so all done by post.

Another surprise I had was the opportunity to gain formal qualifications. After two years of study, I became a fully qualified funeral director, entitling me to have 'Dip FD' after my name, and became a member of the Institute of Funeral Directors. I was invited to attend the annual conference of the institute to collect my certificate which I initially declined, but when they told me it was being held in Guernsey, I quickly changed my mind! Taking the car, we took the Brittany ferry from Poole and had a very pleasant three days on the island, including a lavish dinner for the presentation of the certificates.

Having worked so many evenings and weekends on the course, I considered the possibility of also doing a two-year course on embalming. If I was to set up my own business, this would be a useful skill to have but, as I wasn't considering this at the time, I did not take this further.

Looking back on my career, I am surprised how long I was involved with the funeral trade. Not just twenty years with a company, but immediately on my retirement, continuing on an occasional basis for another ten years, arranging and conducting funerals with the help of a funeral directors in Uckfield, who provided the coffin, vehicles, and bearers. I was even to run their office for a couple of weeks whilst they went on a well earnt holiday. Even now, I get asked for advice on funerals. And with the children being used to conversations about death and the many practical steps needed to be taken to arrange a funeral, they also have been able to help others who had to arrange a funeral. This even extended to helping someone publish a book involving death. The author was assured they had no problem in discussing such details.

A funeral is a significant event for any family, both emotionally and visually: Pomp and circumstance are often involved. From the funeral director's point of view, having smartly dressed staff acting in a dignified manner at all stages of the funeral is important as is the attention to detail of each aspect of the funeral. Behind the scenes is where much of the work is done, though, unseen by the family. Collecting the deceased from a nursing home, for example, was normally done after dark, unobserved by family, neighbours, and even other patients. Even in a private home, after the goodbyes, one would invite the family to go into another room so they would not witness the practical steps we needed to take in order to place the deceased onto a stretcher and take them to the waiting ambulance.

The very first essential task was to place an identity wristlet and a name tag on the deceased to ensure there was never a misidentification of a body. Then came moving the body. Lifting a deceased person could depress the lungs causing a yawning noise which may make the family think the person was still alive. They could also exude a very unpleasant smell. Then there was the lifting once the body was in place, perhaps requiring the stretcher to be upended to negotiate a tight bend in a passageway or staircase. A more modern hazard was getting round stair lifts which made the staircase both narrow and awkward to negotiate. Something the family were often anxious to give to me was the deceased's dentures! With my experience in the dental trade this was not a problem, but I was surprised how often I saw that the wrong teeth had been set in the denture. Extra molars added to fill up the space, for instance! Or, how worn they were; the plastic teeth absolutely flattened through wear.

Back at the funeral parlour, I always made sure their eyes were closed and hair done in case the family wanted to come in to view the deceased. 'If that was my mother' was the standard I set. Then we may have the challenge of dressing the deceased, if their clothes had been brought in. I always requested underwear to be supplied as I felt it important the deceased was dressed correctly. If rigor mortis had set in it was not an easy task.

There were occasions where it would be very unpleasant for the family to view the deceased because of the extent of their injuries leading to the death. A traffic accident, or a suicide off Beachy Head maybe. However, the opportunity to say goodbye is very important, so we had to take steps to appropriately cover the damaged area. Even just to be able to hold their hand could be so helpful for grieving loved ones. And the use of stage makeup and powder helped restore their appearance. Yet another skill I had to learn.

I realise it might be helpful to go further back into my history to explain how I became equipped to, ultimately, run the business more or less by myself, with complete independence and responsibility over the decisions I made.

From the age of eight I was sent to a boarding school, and came home only once a fortnight for four hours on a Sunday. At senior school I was at Bembridge on the Isle of Wight. I was away from home for up to three months at a time. This gave me the experience and confidence to cope on my own and make my own decisions. Looking back on it, how I survived for twenty years working in a factory with three hundred staff, I do not know. But the factory work did give me the opportunity to earn a good wage, eventually enabling us to buy our lovely Sussex cottage. And this location enabled me to join the local funeral director office in Lewes.

Telling people that I was a funeral director was a conversation stopper; death is not a topic most people want to talk about after all. But then I would also be asked about any amusing or difficult experiences I may have had. It would have been indiscrete to tell people most of them though, as regular parts of our job would horrify them. Our training and experience over the years enabled us to cope, together with the support of our work colleagues. Also, there was no option. It was our job. There were some very unpleasant experiences, it's true, but also huge satisfaction in achieving a well organised funeral to meet the expectations of the family.

The title of this memoir, 'Even While They Sleep', comes from Psalms 127 v 2 which reads '*God can provide for his devoted lovers, even while they sleep.*' Considering the way I was led into this business it seems a natural summary of what my role was to be: to look after both the deceased and the family left behind. It is a profession I am proud to have been involved in and from which I got so much satisfaction. I hope that this book will serve as a way to give people some background for what goes on behind the scenes and answer some of the questions I was often asked. And, of course, to recount some of those amusing experiences which I recall, and the really difficult occasions that I have had to overcome.

2.

THE DAILY ROUTINE

Despite what I have entitled this chapter, every day was different depending on what had to be arranged or carried out. Whatever the demands, they always resulted in huge satisfaction at achieving a job well done, though.

A diary was an essential part of daily life. It could be blank four weeks ahead, but you knew you would, in actuality, be busy. Normally, a funeral could be arranged to take place within a fortnight of the death happening. In that two-week period, you could be in the process of arranging and conducting perhaps eight other funerals, all at different stages of arrangement, and all needing close personal contact with the client. The most funerals I arranged to take place in one week was thirteen. This occurred shortly after Christmas one year. It was quite extraordinary how it seemed the very ill hung on until Christmas and then let go. January was always a busy month.

You knew there would be a funeral to arrange after we had been called out to do what we termed 'a removal.' That is, to collect a deceased person, whether that be from a home, a hospital, or a nursing home. There were occasions when the funeral was to take place in another part of the country, in which case our role would be to take the deceased up to the local funeral director. On the other hand, it could be we had to collect the deceased from another part of the country or even an airport if it was a repatriation. We collected bodies from Heathrow, Gatwick, and Bournemouth airports at one time or another. However, more commonly, the death occurred in a hospital or hospice, so the first we knew about it was when a family came into the office or telephoned us to say they wished to make the arrangements. This could be in our office or in their own home, if requested. One unusual home arrangement was when I was asked by a family to visit their home in a village north of Cambridge. After completing the arrangement, I drove to Addenbrooke's Hospital in Cambridge where the deceased was and brought him back to Lewes to make ready for him to be buried in Ringmer. Quite a long-distance affair!

Now, my first amusing story relates to this arrangement I made in Cambridgeshire. One of the ladies who was arranging the funeral with me was holding a young baby. She decided that he needed changing and, taking the wet nappy off, she gave me the baby to hold while she went to collect a clean nappy. You can guess what happened next. The cold air got to him and he promptly weed on my lap; laughter all round.

Another memory was when we went to Heathrow Airport to collect a coffin. It was brought out of the warehouse on a forklift truck contained in a large wooden packing case. No way would that fit into the hearse, nor had we come prepared to take a case apart. We asked the driver of the forklift truck to help. "Can't do that - against union rules," was his response. However, a substantial donation effected a change of heart and an hour later we were off back to Lewes.

Being prepared to speak to a client day or night was important, pen and paper ready to take down the details. I was once asked to give a quotation for a funeral at 10 o'clock at night before the client could decide which funeral director to choose. When gathering the initial information, it was very important to get the name right. For example, was the name spelt 'Elizabeth Stuart,' or 'Elisabeth Stewart'? If we were requested to collect the deceased from a private home we would ask if a doctor had confirmed the death and who the doctor was. This is because we did, very occasionally, get hoax calls. Twice I was called to what turned out to be a fictitious address. On one occasion the young lady who answered the door told us she had already had the fire brigade and an ambulance call at her house. Well, now a funeral director, too. She was so distressed. It seemed she had just broken up with her boyfriend and it was he who was making these hoax calls. For the two of us in the removal car, getting up in the middle of the night without a purpose was very annoying. Two hours of wasted time and no sleep.

As most people have never arranged a funeral before, you have to guide them through all the necessary procedures and ensure they are made aware of all the different choices available to them: cremation or burial; a faith-based service; a humanist funeral, or a non-faith service using a celebrant. If it was a cremation, did they want a church service before coming to the crematorium or perhaps a memorial service following the cremation? Then they had to decide the coffin type, the transport required, hymns and music, orders of service, obituary notices, floral tributes, and other such items. Our aim was to make the funeral they have arranged as personal and meaningful as possible. It was then up to us to meet those expectations. Anger is one of the common emotions of the bereaved, so any hiccup or mistake is likely to be met with extreme ire. At the end of the second funeral arrangement I ever made, the family said to me, "It's nice to leave it to the experts." Fortunately, all went well.

"I have the death certificate" a family would often inform me. It may be a surprise when I tell you, there is no such thing. There is a 'Certificate of Cause of Death' issued by the doctor and a 'Certificate for Burial or Cremation' issued by the Registrar. The exception to this is when the death has been referred to the coroner when he will issue an 'Electronic' certificate to allow the funeral to go ahead.

A cremation normally takes a longer time to fix a date than a burial due to more documentation required and, depending how busy the crematorium was and the time slots available, what date would be suitable for the family. A burial could be carried out in as little as two days, although normally it would take about a week. Beware if the date of a funeral had to be changed. It can cause quite the upset because, 'Oh no! I have informed all the family now,' or, 'We have already booked the venue for the wake!' The other need for urgency was when a family had flown from another country to see their ill relative who had died. They would then want to stay for the funeral but would generally have already booked a date to fly back home.

A procedure which changed significantly was getting the BCF form, stating the cause or causes of death, completed. This form is necessary for a cremation to go ahead and has to be signed by two doctors. If the deceased died in hospital or a hospice, no problem. If the deceased was already in our mortuary, we had to arrange for the doctor to call in. After the case of Dr Shipman who engineered deaths and did not disclose to the second doctor that anything was amiss, the law was changed so that the second doctor also had to contact the family to ensure they were happy with the cause of death stated on the form. It could be quite upsetting for many families as it raised suspicions that possibly not all was quite right. This form was then sent to the crematorium where a third doctor would finally authorise for the cremation to go ahead. Only once did we have an occasion where the crematorium requested a post-mortem. The date was set for the funeral and all the family had made preparations to attend. We spoke to the son and he agreed that the funeral should still go ahead on the day arranged so as not to upset the family, only there would be no committal prayer said. Two days later, the son attended the committal by himself.

So, the funeral has been arranged. Now for the preparations behind the scenes. First, sending written confirmation to the family and to the minister taking the funeral. Then phoning through the obituary notices and ordering the flowers and orders of service. If it was to be a burial, you must book the grave digger, and contact the memorial mason if an existing headstone had to be removed. Then there was the internal work to organise. Whilst we had a stock of popular coffin styles – or perhaps I should say the most commonly chosen - we had to order the larger sizes on demand. They may sometimes have to be custom made, as was the case for a 42 stone individual. The lining of the coffin and fixing of the coffin handles we did ourselves, as well as fixing a crucifix to the lid of a Roman Catholic coffin and engraving the name plate. In the early days in the business, we offered cheap plywood coffins covered with felt, ones with a printed wood design, a wood veneered coffin, a solid oak coffin, a woven willow coffin or - nightmare - a cardboard coffin. How could you ever make a cardboard coffin look nice - a body displayed in a cardboard box! And, if the cardboard creases, that will always be a weak spot where the coffin could start to fold. Not a good experience when carrying the coffin into a service! Plus, if cardboard gets wet it loses its strength entirely. I really did not approve of them. Since I retired, though, many more choices of coffin are now available. You want the emblem of your favourite football club on the side? Perhaps a floral design? No problem! A funeral director's price list I saw recently offered a choice of 30 different coffins. I do believe these new options are a real improvement on personalising the coffin. The older styles were quite Victorian in character.

Another duty we had to undertake was to prepare and dress the deceased. We would ensure the deceased's eyes were closed, and small clear eye caps were placed under the eyelids as on death the eyes go flat. Placing these eye caps restores the shape of the eye and makes the person look just asleep. Their hair would be done and sometimes a stage type powder put on the face to help improve appearance. I once had a formal complaint made against me for the way the man's wife's hair looked. He had provided a photograph of his wife when she was in good health, where she had the most beautiful long locks. However, after many months of serious illness, her hair was lacklustre and no way was it possible to restore its original beauty. To the grieving husband, it just added to his distress.

The other task involved closing the mouth. When someone dies, it is helpful to put some support under the jaw to help the mouth to stay closed. After rigor mortis has set in, some artificial way of closing the mouth must be used which requires the lower jaw to be sewn to the upper jaw. I won't go into details of how it is done but it is essential for the deceased to be presented to the family in an acceptable way. Some funeral directors did not have this skill and used plastic props under the chin. The problem was, these could often be seen by those viewing the deceased.

Unless the family provided clothing for the deceased, we would dress the deceased in a white, blue, or pink gown. Perhaps the most personal task was to remove jewellery. We learnt a technique for removing a tight-fitting ring from a finger without damaging the skin: by placing a length of cotton under the ring and then twisting round and round the finger it allowed the skin to slip under the ring and it could then be safely removed.

There were occasions when we were requested to take the deceased back to their home prior to the funeral. Carrying a deceased in a coffin into a house could be quite difficult. Getting round corners or up the stairs could be challenging. And then, if the coffin was to stay open, it required us to visit the house daily to ensure all was well. One would not like unpleasant smells or discolouring to become apparent; it would be upsetting for the family to experience.

When all preparations had been made and confirmations sent out, the next task was to plan the day. This involved questions such as what vehicles were required? Often it would be a hearse only, direct to the crematorium where the family would meet us. They could follow the hearse from their home in their own vehicles or they could ask for the full cortège from the home to where the service was to be held. If more than two limousines were requested, we had to hire in limousines from other funeral directors.

In my early days I did most of the preparations myself and

hired casual staff - mainly retired men - to clean and drive the vehicles and to bear the coffin, and diligent they were. It was important to use men of approximately the same height to ensure the coffin was carried level and evenly. One short person and the other three had all the weight. It was surprising the number of widowers who came to us after we had done a funeral for their wives, to ask to become a casual bearer. We did use a number of them, and they were very dedicated but tended to stay with us only for a short time. It was a way for them to work through their grief. For most funerals, we needed four bearers to carry the coffin, but for a larger coffin, six bearers. The most I saw was ten for a 42 stone gentleman who had to be lowered into a grave – more on his funeral later.

Training those staff was vital so that they knew how to lift, carry, and lower a coffin correctly. Clear instruction from the funeral director was paramount, particularly if you were working with an inexperienced team or an experienced team from another company who were used to working in a different way from what I expected. Planned and clear instructions were the way to go. Once, we nearly had a serious problem carrying a coffin out of a bedroom where the deceased had laid prior to the funeral. Normally, two bearers should be at each end of the coffin to take the weight. On this occasion an inexperienced bearer came back into the room leaving a lady bearer by herself at the other end taking the weight of the heavy coffin. How we stopped the coffin crashing to the ground with all the family watching proceedings I don't know.

To drive the hearse or limousine, you should always prioritise a gentle start or slowing down. I remember two problem drivers I had. One, an ex-bus driver: start quickly and brake fast was his style. The other was an ex driving instructor. He drove so close to the curb he hit every drain cover, so the limousine bounced from one drain to the next. In the hearse, clear instructions were vital. 'Follow that yellow car,' I told one driver just as another yellow car drove past. He swerved to the left until I shouted 'not that one, *that* one!' Anticipating traffic lights in order to keep the cortege together could always be a challenge. Certainly not a case of 'let's see if we can make it.' More the case of allowing it to change before you got there so you knew that, when the lights turned green, you could get the whole cortège through. Turning into Lewes Cemetery required careful instructions to the following cars as the turn off is in the middle of a set of traffic lights. If the lights turned red before all the cars had come through, those remaining would not see us turn off and, when the lights turned green, they would carry on up the hill, searching for us and the cemetery. We always informed the traffic warden of potential traffic hold ups.

It was important to behave appropriately and respectfully at the church or crematorium whilst standing by the hearse, waiting to carry the coffin in. There was the need to keep quiet if waiting outside while the service was in progress because it could be very quiet inside during a church service and to hear staff outside conversing and laughing away was not acceptable. I later insisted the bearers came into a church service. One, to keep control of everything and two, to help with the singing, which many enjoyed. I had one new hearse driver who told me he did not wish to stay in during church services. 'Then you are off the funeral,' I told him. 'You can't do that!' he replied, 'I'm the hearse driver.' 'No, I can drive the hearse. Bye.' Unsurprisingly, he came in.

Carrying a coffin into a church could have its difficulties. Newhaven Parish Church has a long carry in and there are several steps. On one occasion, with the men carrying a heavy coffin, I had to interrupt the minister whilst he was intoning the normal processional verses to ask him to speed up as the men would likely collapse under the weight. At Berwick Church there was also a long carry in over a gravel path, whilst at Hellingly it had a very uneven brick path. Services at St Anne's Church in Lewes required parking on double white lines, so we always forewarned the local traffic warden. Ringmer and Claydon Churches were among many who had low entrances which required the bearers to underhand the coffin through the entrance before again raising it to their shoulders. Among the crematoriums we visited, Downs Crematorium in Brighton was difficult as there are a number of steps to negotiate before entering the chapel. With the increasing number of obese people, a need grew to make families aware of this problem before they decided on which crematorium to choose. I always insisted floral tributes on the coffin were tied on as they could easily slide off while carrying the coffin up a slope. On one occasion at the Downs, a 'DAD' floral arrangement was asked to be placed on the coffin. It slipped off and crashed on the floor, breaking into bits. 'I knew my father never loved me,' exclaimed the daughter. Not a nice experience.

I found there was a greater difference between one minister and another than there ever was between one denomination and another. Some had a natural gift of empathising with the congregation, others were in their own world. Some seemed to put on a special solemn voice for the service which came across as most unnatural. It probably did not help that the minister had never met the deceased, so relied on the family's remembrances. And knowing some of the deceased myself, I often wondered who the minister was talking about. Their words bore no resemblance to the person I knew.

The length of time the minister took varied, but individuals tended to follow the same pattern each time. One lovely, retired minister we used regularly at Brighton took fourteen minutes every time. Twenty minutes was around normal at a crematorium. Half to three-quarters of an hour for a church service. The record for a church service? Eight and a half minutes, including singing 'All Things Bright and Beautiful.' There were a number of times the minister forgot to close the curtain at the end of the crematorium service. I just went up, bowed to the coffin, and ushered the family out as if it was the normal procedure. Two ministers we used regularly included the same messages each time. One, who lived under the South Downs, always introduced his talk with the first two verses of Psalm 121: *'I lift up my eyes to the hills, where does my help come from.'* He then added that every time he came out of his house and saw the Downs, he remembered that verse and the one that follows it: *'My help comes from the Lord, the Maker of heaven and earth.'* Talking to, probably, many local to his parish, he immediately had the congregation identifying with him and his message. The second minister's message was simpler and was included at the end of his talk: *'And it is in the message of Easter that we have our hope.'*

At strict Baptist churches the services took much longer, with a three-quarter hour sermon not uncommon. Proceedings were all very formal. One chapel actually stopped using us when our company decided we would drive grey vehicles and wear grey suits: only black was considered suitable to them.

Moving on to graves, let me first explain the difference between a cemetery and a churchyard. A cemetery may be run by the local counsel or a private company. With cemeteries you are likely to be able to choose any design of memorial you would like, and grave spaces can be purchased and reserved for years ahead. In a churchyard, the choice of headstone is more restricted. For example, no marble, no lead lettering, and on granite memorials - a popular choice - a polished surface was not permitted, only an eggshell finish. Also, grave spaces in a churchyard cannot be purchased or reserved ahead unless a special faculty was applied for and that was rarely given. Another factor regarding churchyards is that most are already full, particularly in towns. So, if a burial is requested, there is often no option but to choose a cemetery. Increasingly available are woodland burial sites. These are advertised as more environmentally friendly, being in natural settings that are free from traditional memorials and tributes found in a cemetery.

Staying on the subject of graves, each churchyard could have different difficulties when digging the grave. At Hamsey, there are enormous flint stones embedded in the chalk, making it hard work to dig. At Laughton, in winter, the water table could be so high that water would have to be pumped out of the ground, sometimes up to just prior to the end of the service. On one occasion, it had just been pumped out prior to lowering the coffin into the grave and, by the time the minister had finished the committal, the coffin had floated to the level of the ground. The service completed, the water was pumped out again, the coffin sunk down to the bottom, and the grave filled in. At the adjoining parish of Ripe, the problem here is the ground is fine sand. If the grave was dug too early, the sides just crumbled in. The grave digging could not be completed until the service was nearly over!

There is one particular incident of a collapsing grave in my memory that could have been upsetting for the family had they witnessed it. The church service completed, the coffin was carried to the grave and placed on the putlocks – wooden beams supporting the coffin over the grave. But, due to the weight of the coffin, the soft ground started to collapse and began to fill the grave. 'Quick,' I said, 'lower the coffin in before the family arrives." The committal proceeded as normal. However, when the family had departed, we had to lift the coffin out again because it had only gone down a couple of feet and the grave was meant to be a double depth; in other words, there had to be room for a second coffin to go in at some later time.

Another incident I recall happened at Wilmington Cemetery. We had often attended there but, on this occasion, for the first time, the grave was on a different side of the main path. The committal was completed and the family moved away, however the cemetery attendant had not told us that the coffins were to face the opposite direction to those above the path. Why were we not told? The family, unaware of the problem, were ushered back to the limousines and left, enabling us to lift the coffin out, turn it round and lower it again. Would it have mattered? Well, later when a head stone was added, it would otherwise have been placed at the foot of the coffin, not the head.

The weather also created difficulties, illustrated by this experience we had at Woodingdean Cemetery, situated right on top of the Downs near Brighton. The church service had been completed and we had arrived at the cemetery for the burial to take place. The coffin was placed on to the putlocks ready for burial, and all the floral tributes laid nearby for the family to view after the committal. It was a very windy day and suddenly an extreme gust of wind came and lifted all the tributes into the air and carried them across the adjoining fields, never to be seen again.

Everyone has their trade secrets, and I had a special trick at the graveside. When the minister came to the 'ashes to ashes' part of the committal, I always had some sand in my hand to symbolically scatter on the coffin. One day, a mourner came up to me to say she had often seen me do this but never saw me pick up any soil to scatter on the coffin. How did I do it? I revealed to her that I always had a small plastic container in my pocket filled with sand, so, at a discreet moment, I poured the sand into my hand ready to scatter on the coffin. Just one of the many duties a funeral director has to plan for.

Lastly, for this chapter, I once had the privilege of doing the funeral of a 102-year-old lady whose request it was to be buried with her husband who had died some eighty years before, aged just 22. Thankfully, we managed to find the grave in Rodmell Churchyard, so her wishes were met, much to our satisfaction.

A farmer's farewell journey on his trailer complete with ploughshears, milkchurns, and hay bales

3.

THOSE SPECIAL OCCASIONS

Perhaps I should clarify, to begin with, that I firmly believe that all funerals are special occasions. To the family certainly, and to me. Trying to ensure that everything goes right and the family have been able to express their grief in the way they wanted, made each funeral a special occasion. I carried out this privileged task over five thousand times in my years as a funeral director!

However, there are many funerals I arranged which have special memories or were new experiences for me. For example, the different denominations I attended to. I have many memories of these.

We had a Russian Orthodox funeral at Downs Crematorium. A double slot had been booked because of the length of the service and the minister was clothed in his magnificent ceremonial robes. Whilst much of the service was in Russian, he explained at each stage what the prayers were and the significance of the procedures he undertook.

The Greek Orthodox Church of the Holy Trinity in Brighton is magnificent inside. The ornate altar is set behind an equally ornate screen and it reminded me of the biblical Holy of Holies. A funeral service I recall here included an elaborate communion with much incense burnt and the bells used for Mass being rung.

We had a similar experience at St Andrew Bobola Roman Catholic Polish Church in Hammersmith, London. My memory here is of the many candles lit around the entire church. The service was followed by a burial at Barnes Cemetery and, after the burial, we took the family in our limousine to the wake. Here the family got into a conversation with a long-lost friend of the deceased and offered him a lift back to his home, in Barnet! An hour and a half further north in what was, by now, the evening rush hour. We then had to take the family back to Hailsham. It turned out to be a very long day covering over two hundred and fifty miles.

Rounding off the Roman Catholic theme, we conducted a funeral of a Catholic minister in Our Lady of Ransom in Eastbourne. There were dozens of other Catholic ministers involved in the service and so much incense was burnt that you could not see the altar. It was quite a grand service.

One extremely memorable funeral came in 1994. I arranged the funeral of Fanny Craddock, the well-known English restaurant critic, television cook, and writer. The service was to take place at Eastbourne Crematorium, where she would be cremated. As I stepped out of the hearse to lead it to the chapel, I noticed television cameras trained on me. I did my best to walk with dignity despite being hindered by heavy rain and a strong wind blowing. It was a real struggle, but later, watching it back on the news broadcast, I think it looked okay.

Fanny — No one saw the last show

RIGHT:
Fanny Craddock in her heyday

BELOW:
She had only a handful of mourners

Credit: Eastbourne Herald

MILLIONS watched Fanny Craddock at the height of her TV cookshow fame, but just a handful of mourners attended her funeral in Sussex yesterday.

Fewer than 20 people turned up for a private service at Eastbourne Crematorium, just a couple of miles from the Brsham Nursing Home, in Hailsham, where she died.

The ashes of the screen celebrity, who passed away on December 27 at the age of 84, will be scattered with those of her late husband, Johnny, under a rose bush at the crematorium.

Speaking before the service, her solicitor, Christopher Doman, described the larger-than-life star as a true fighter.

Mr Doman said: "She never ceased to be a strong character and had remarkable strength of character right until the end."

Mr Doman, who works for Thomas, Eggar, Verrall & Bowles, in Chichester, said it had always been the star's wish to have a simple ceremony.

He added: "When she was well she was her old self, but she did have periods when she was extremely ill.

"She almost died a couple of years ago, but managed to pull through. She was not in very good health for some time and I think there were a number of things wrong.

"In the end, old age got the better of her."

Fanny's performances were the talk of the day for 20 years and she regularly appeared with husband Johnny by her side until the show was axed in the Seventies.

Her former neighbour and friend, the Rev Tenniel Evans, from Beaconsfield, in Buckinghamshire, said behind the scenes the star was a very different person to the TV personality many knew.

He said: "I knew Fanny for 50 years and her bark was far worse than her bite. A lot of people had cows with her, but she was a wonderful woman."

Credit: Eastbourne Herald

Television crew and the press were much in evidence at the funeral of Fanny Craddock which I conducted in 1995.

Another occasion at Eastbourne Cemetery was a funeral I arranged for an eighteen-year-old boy who had a particular passion for aircraft and cars. The main family tribute on the coffin was a floral car. But what made this occasion so special was, as the curtains were closing and silence reigned in the chapel, the jets of the RAF Red Arrow Display Team roared low overhead. It was the Eastbourne Air Show that day and the noise was deafening. Seconds before and it would have interrupted the service. The timing was a perfect send off for a boy who loved aircraft. I had so many comments later asking me how had I arranged that? Just one of my many skills apparently!

An odd similarity occurred at the scattering of ashes of this same boy's father a couple of years later. His ashes were to be scattered near the cricket pitch where he had once played. Just as we completed the ceremony, the clouds gently parted, revealing a vintage de Havilland Venom gracefully soaring overhead as if paying a final, elegant tribute from the skies. The symbolism of this event, so similar to his son's, was not lost on the family.

Another aircraft related event occurred during the summer airshow week at an ashes interment in Langney Cemetery. Only the widow, her four-year-old grandson, and the vicar were present. As the vicar was intoning the prayers of committal, the Lancaster and a Spitfire of the Battle of Britain Memorial Flight flew low overhead. 'Look, Granny, look,' shouted the boy, pulling at Granny's arm, quite drowning out the sound of the vicar. One could only smile.

What should have been a special event for a family, but went terribly awry, was a funeral I arranged to be carried out in a crematorium north of Norwich, in Norfolk. We took the deceased up to an associate branch in Norwich and it was they who carried out the funeral. The family drove up from Sussex and arrived at the crematorium an hour early. Having found out where it was, they drove off back to Norwich for a coffee. Unfortunately, on their return, they found the road had been closed for emergency repairs. They eventually arrived as the service ended! The vicar had persuaded the remaining mourners, probably with the encouragement of the crematorium staff, to go ahead with the funeral without the main mourners present! Not a good decision. The family were certainly upset, but fortunately I could not get the blame.

Another distant funeral I arranged involved driving a hearse and two limousines to Ipswich Crematorium in Suffolk. On the evening before the funeral, it snowed heavily, so I contacted the family to suggest we leave two hours earlier than planned to ensure we arrived on time. It was slow driving up through Tunbridge Wells but then it began to clear, and beyond the Dartford tunnel the roads were clear. So, with time on our hands, I directed the cortège into a Little Chef near Colchester. The family were happy to stop and have breakfast, which they treated us to, as well. After the cremation we took the family to a local pub for the wake and, again, we were invited to join in. Can you enjoy a funeral? Certainly, this was quite a pleasant event for us.

This next instance involved a rather challenging task: how to bury someone who weighed forty-two stone. Our first step was to collect the deceased from the hospital. We arrived at the mortuary to find the deceased was still in a hospital bed. They did not have a trolley strong enough to take him, so they had to wheel the whole bed from the ward to the mortuary. With help, we managed to transfer him to our stretcher and place him in the ambulance. A strong, oversized coffin was ordered, and its size passed on to a surprised grave digger. On the day of the funeral, we had to borrow an industrial trolley to take the weight. We drove up in the hearse taking the floral tributes but then used a van to take up the coffin and trolley. We arrived well before the funeral service began in the church to enable us to lower the coffin into the grave before the family arrived. We thought it would not be suitable for the family to see us using the industrial trolley to take the coffin to the graveside or witness the ten of us lowering the coffin into the grave. This was in case a problem occurred with the grave size or in the lowering of such a huge coffin. It was certainly a snug fit, and there was no way we'd have been able to lift it out again. The church service followed, and the minister carried out the normal committal at the graveside.

The following of convention is not, always, at the forefront of everyone's minds. I once experienced an elderly vicar who led a funeral service in the chapel at a local cemetery. Afterwards we carried the coffin to the graveside but, before we could remove the floral tribute on the coffin or thread the webbing for lowering the coffin into the grave, the vicar began to read the committal. He duly finished it and got straight back into his car and drove off before we had even placed the coffin over the grave. Luckily most people are probably not aware of procedures at the graveside and, certainly, the family did not seem to notice his early departure. At least the cemetery had provided putlocks to place the coffin on before lowering. When we first used this cemetery, they didn't have putlocks and it was only after a member of our staff had fallen into a grave whilst trying to carry a coffin that they used them. Maybe because our company donated a pair!

Quaker funerals were always special, with a real sincerity in all that was said and done. Mostly these were conducted in silence but with the occasional contribution by a member of the congregation. The service ended with the leader standing up and then all shook hands and left the chapel. I arranged one Quaker funeral in Barking, where Elizabeth Fry was buried. It was the only Quaker funeral service I ever attended where a hymn was sung.

It was often the little incidences at funerals that became special memories to me. With one funeral cortège leaving from a house in Polegate to go to Eastbourne Crematorium, the family were eager to leave although I had said there was plenty of time. Consequently, I paged the hearse away – when the funeral director walks in front of the hearse as a mark of respect for the deceased - for perhaps two hundred yards to use up time. The family complimented me later on what dignity that had added to the funeral.

Another early arrival was because the address was in Portslade, and I had not had the opportunity to check out the location so we set off early in case of delays. With a hearse and two limousines, we drove past the house with a quarter of an hour to spare and decided to park up. However, we saw the family had seen us and were all pouring out of the house and waved to us to come down. On arrival I told them we were early, but they had already set the house alarm, they said, so could we get going. This particular funeral also stands out because when we arrived at the church in Brighton, having carried the coffin in and shown the family to their seats, the minister immediately announced the hymn. However, no hymn books had been put out and, as there was no verger present, I had to scurry to the back of the church to look through various cupboards for the books. The family just about managed to join in in time to sing the last verse.

Conversely, some funerals can be remembered for a very late start. We arrived at one particular house in good time with a hearse and two limousines. As I went into the house, cups of tea were being handed out to the assembled family including the grandfather who sat near the door. Ten minutes later I was starting to urge the family to make their way to the limousines. 'It's all right,' said the grandfather, 'we've still got ten minutes.' Time had not moved on for him. Finally, the tea was drunk. All ready? No, one of the mourners could not find her shoes and had to open a cupboard by the front door, blocking the exit. Further delay. Then the front doorbell rang and some long-lost relative arrived to a big welcome. More delay as hellos were said all round. The funeral was booked for 1.00pm at the crematorium which meant I would normally leave a half hour before. We left at 12.55pm! This resulted in a slightly faster journey down than was normal, as you can imagine.

I was, at another time, privileged to conduct the funeral of the boss of Harvey's Brewery, the oldest independent brewery in Sussex. The service was in the Roman Catholic Church in Lewes and was attended by a very large congregation including many dignitaries. However, the minister had to apologise during the service because of the racket coming from next door. It was from a Harvey's pub and the noise came from the metal beer casks they were unloading. It was so appropriate that it brought a big laugh from everyone.

A favourite memory of mine is about an incident which occurred at Hamsey Church, near Lewes. It is believed to be built around 975 AD and it perches on a small hill almost entirely surrounded by the River Ouse. Access is over a narrow bridge and through a farmyard. On this occasion we had warned the farmer to ensure we could get through. 'No problem,' was his response. However, when we arrived, a council dustcart was parked in the yard and our immaculate hearse and limousine had to squeeze through the farmyard slurry to get past.

Pulling up at the churchyard, we opened the rear of the hearse ready to take out the coffin. It was then that a collie dog came up and laid a stone at our feet, waiting with great expectation for us to throw it. We duly ignored it and started to carry the coffin to the grave, but the collie continued to run ahead of us and put the stone down for us to throw. Again, we duly ignored it. The coffin was finally placed on the putlocks over the grave and the minister started the burial service. I looked down and saw that the collie had actually placed the stone on my shoe, his nose quivering inches away. I looked up to see all the family looking at me, not the minister. When the minister completed the committal, I asked the family what I should do. 'Throw it,' they told me, which I did. They then told me that the deceased had had a dog which did exactly that and he would have loved this little episode. The family were delighted.

Credit: Nick Macneill

St Peter's Church, Hamsey. This small 'island' church can be seen on a low mound some two miles north of Lewes.

On the topic of animals, one of the options available at a funeral is to release white doves. These would arrive in a wicker basket and would be released at the graveside. In theory they would then fly home, but occasionally one would hang around for a few days. Anyway, on one occasion, as they were released, they all flew over the vicar in his white cassock, showering him with their droppings.

Unusual happenings are par for the course as a funeral director. I recall that on two occasions I had to arrange double funerals where the husband and wife died within a day of each other. Both were cremations and we used two hearses to process into the crematorium.

I also arranged funerals for some very intriguing individuals including one with a lady who worked with the Ministry of Defence during the war as a secretary. Whilst alive she told me of a meeting she was present at where she took the minutes during the decision to change the name of the V1 bomb from a 'Pilotless Aircraft' to a 'Doodlebug.' They thought the title Pilotless Aircraft was too alarming for the general public.

Another gentleman I met when arranging a funeral was someone who had piloted a midget submarine during the war and had lain off the D-Day beaches just before the invasion in June 1944.

I also got to see some interesting sights. One house I visited had a number of superb dioramas of Britains lead soldiers set out in amazing scenes. At another house, I spotted an old Trix model engine on the sideboard. On completing the arrangement, I asked about it. The gentleman immediately offered to show me his train set up stairs. It filled two rooms. He had made all the track, points, and electric signals himself and he could run seven trains simultaneously! There was no scenery, it was just a superb exercise in electronics. Our electrician, when he called recently at my home, recalled he had visited that same address some thirty years ago and even as a qualified electrician, was astonished at the complexity of the work.

It was not always a house we were called to collect a deceased from. It could be from a caravan, out in the garden, or even the countryside. Removals from hotels could be interesting. Entry and exit were always by the back door and along back passages normally reserved for staff. Grand entrances sometimes gave way to narrow passages often leading to surprisingly small bedrooms. Obviously converted at some time or another to maximise the number of guests the hotel could accommodate. When the coroner called, we could be going anywhere. Such occasions are worth a chapter of its own.

In all, I probably attended over two hundred different churches, chapels, and crematoriums in the course of my career as a funeral director, each one different, each one special.

Paging the hearse down the busy A22 with police escort

4.

OUT IN THE DARK

Being a funeral director is a twenty-four-hour business and it was many a dark evening that I had to go out to collect a deceased person. Nursing and care homes would nearly always ask you to come late in the evening to ensure the rest of their patients were in bed and to avoid neighbours seeing what was going on. 'Use the back door please!'

When the telephone went at night, I think the caller thought you were sitting at a desk, all ready and waiting. not deep asleep in bed. It was important to have paperwork always at hand, as you must write down all the necessary information. This was before the age of satnav, so I first had to look in a map book to find the address, then telephone my colleague who was on duty as well and arrange where to meet. Then get dressed and head off out, hoping the car windscreen was not iced up and it was not foggy. If it was a night call from the coroner's officer, they would expect us to attend within half an hour, so ensuring everything was at hand, including socks, shoes, coat, and the car keys, was vital.

Finding the address could be difficult to do. You were often driving down long driveways or along rutted farm tracks hoping you were in the right place. Even modern estates in towns tend to have lots of twittens leading off between houses where even more houses can be found. Once, in Hailsham, we had driven around the estate three times before a police car drew up to ask what we were about. Someone had reported a suspicious car cruising around. We told them our mission and eventually found the address. Then, when we were coming away from an address in Polegate once, the fog had become so thick that we drove around the estate twice before spotting the exit.

When the doctor was able to confirm the cause of death, the deceased was taken back to the local office, so we were likely to be back home in about an hour and a half. Following a coroner's call, we would have to take the deceased either to Eastbourne District General Hospital or The Royal Sussex County Hospital, depending on which part of the county the death had occurred in. We would have to obtain the keys to the mortuary, open up, undress the deceased, and place them into the refrigerators. Such trips were more likely to take at least two hours.

It is perhaps sad that people believed they had to take action immediately if someone had died. I think it would have been beneficial for them to say their goodbyes in their own time with the deceased in their natural environment, in their home, in their bed. After the doctor had confirmed death, it seemed that the family were likely to be advised to get the deceased into 'care.' Witnessing a death can be traumatic. The deceased can look unsightly, their mouth wide open. They're likely to have soiled themselves meaning there could be unpleasant smells or discharges. The hair might be a mess and sometimes they're not properly clothed, perhaps still in their pyjamas or even naked if they had, for instance, died in the bath. Where they died can certainly add to the trauma for the loved ones. Sitting on the toilet, in a hotel bedroom where they were holidaying, or, on one occasion, the deceased had died whilst in someone else's bed! Somewhat traumatic. Both for the wife and also the girlfriend. We later conducted the man's funeral and there were rather a number of ladies, all crying copiously!

Having recovered the deceased, we would offer to tidy the body up for the loved ones to say their goodbyes before we took the deceased to our ambulance. Unless forewarned, one never knew the weight of the person you were going to have to lift. And, as mentioned before, there were often difficult passageways and stairs to negotiate, particularly if there was a sharp turn in the stairs requiring us to up end the stretcher to manoeuvre it around. Narrow lifts also meant upending the stretcher. Then, you may have to move valuable china or clocks out of the way to avoid an accident. A particularly difficult removal I had was from the fifth floor of a block of flats when the lift was not working. That was very hard work.

We once had a most unpleasant welcome when, believing we had arrived at the correct address - in this case a stately mansion, we drew up at the main entrance. Flood lights came on, an upstairs window opened, and a man, pointing a gun at us, shouted, 'Want do you want?' We told him that we were funeral directors and had been requested to collect this particular person. 'He lives in the lodge at the entrance,' he replied and slammed the window shut. We turned back down the drive and found the house.

I am not sure if early morning calls were any easier to cope with than calls before midnight, as you may not get a chance to get back home to have a sleep. If you were called out after 3am, by the time all was complete it could be getting light. The milk floats were about, and lorries starting moving. It felt hardly worth getting undressed and climbing back into bed.

If you want to see wildlife though, go into the towns in the middle of the night to see the foxes and rats. Around Newhaven

Port, which is always well lit, the seagulls were always calling and flying around. Driving over the Downs to Seaford I would often see badgers.

When I was returning home late at night in the pitch black, I'd find it so quiet; With no noise from traffic, it was so peaceful. I have heard stories of country places in Africa where the inhabitants of one village could communicate with people in villages on the other side of a valley because it was so quiet. With the peace I experienced here, I could understand that. If you think about it, just over one hundred years ago, before the advent of the combustion engine, this country would have always been as quiet as that. How things have changed.

The biggest fright I had at night was when we collected a deceased person from a nursing home in Eastbourne. We were directed to go around the back and use the fire escape to get to the first floor. All was in pitch black. We opened the tailgate of the car to retrieve the stretcher, leaving it open for easy access upon our return. We ascended the fire escape, retrieved the deceased, and came down to the car again. As we pushed the stretcher in, there was a scratching noise and a black shape shot out. I really screamed. I thought it was the person on the stretcher and they had somehow got out. We saw moments later a black cat stalking away. It must have jumped into the car while we were upstairs.

One of the sadder stories I have heard of was when the ambulance collecting the deceased ran over the deceased's cat. The deceased had left in his will that his entire estate should be used to ensure the cat was looked after properly.

In all my years on the job driving to deaths I only got stopped once by the police. It was on Christmas Eve, and they were checking for drink drivers. I pointed to the deceased in the back, and he quickly let us go.

5.

THE TRAVELLER COMMUNITY

Whilst working at R Butler & Sons I built up a very good rapport with the traveller community. Their funerals always required a lot of time to be committed to them. You had to ensure they knew exactly what was happening at every stage of the funeral from the initial collection of the deceased to the fixing of the gravestone. And these occasions led to many unusual happenings. The travellers would demand a lot but, with their cash payment, you would naturally expect a lot.

Traveller tradition is for the deceased to be returned to their home in the coffin to rest there for four days prior to the burial. Often, this would be a caravan, and getting a coffin through its door was not easy. They sometimes had to cut the doorway wider. That would spoil the caravan but again tradition said that the caravan was burnt after the funeral so it wouldn't be used again.

Getting the coffin into a house, if this was the residence, could also be difficult. If it would not go around a corner, they would simply take the window out to give us access to where the deceased was to be placed. If we couldn't get the hearse near the house? Don't worry, they would dig up the pavement. A fence in the way? It would be moved.

The room in which the coffin was placed was always beautifully prepared. Most of the furniture was removed except for a table or two to take vases of flowers. The walls were lined with white sheets upon which were fastened ribbons and little sprays of flowers.

I would visit the home every day to ensure the deceased remained presentable, making any adjustments necessary. Perhaps some make up, some aerosol spray to overcome possible odour. Even to provide a fresh funeral gown. In the days leading up to the funeral, more and more people turned up and by the previous evening there was likely to be a large gathering of men all around a bonfire outside, the women all inside the house.

Traveller funerals always booked a number of limousines. The most I ever arranged was for fourteen limousines. The challenge was they had to be all black, no grey ones which many funeral companies had started to use. The cortège would consist of a hearse, the limousines, two or three flatbed lorries to take the flowers, and twenty or thirty cars following on behind. Keeping that cortège together was a challenge. We always advised the police, who occasionally were able to provide assistance. Parking around the church for a service certainly caused disruption with so many vehicles, and double white lines were ignored.

You would arrive at the house at least one hour before you were due to leave. The house and surrounding garden would be filled with family and fellow travellers. The first task was to bring the coffin out of the house and place it in front of the house with the lid off. The family would then gather around to say their goodbyes. While this went on, we would start to load the flowers on the flatbed lorries. You had to ensure the cards were secure so that they did not blow away on the journey. Then the floral arrangements themselves had to be tied down to prevent them blowing away also. One hundred and fifty tributes was not unusual.

Ten minutes before you wanted to close up the coffin, you would ask the mourners - probably all men - to move aside as we needed to close the coffin, knowing they would not yet move. Another warning five minutes later but when you really needed to start, you approached the matriarch, always the most important person on any decision. It was like the parting of the Red Sea. The men would immediately move aside, the coffin would be closed, the main tribute tied on, and the coffin loaded into the hearse. I always paged the cortège away with due ceremony

We were expected to drive no more than twenty miles an hour. Traffic lights were ignored; they kept coming, even across the busy A27. Woe betide a protesting car driver complaining - they were quickly advised what to do with themselves! If the service was at the town church the high street would become completely blocked as the cars in the cortège were abandoned along the road.

I warned the vicars that it was most often the men who would show extreme emotions during the service or at the graveside. Normally, two hymns were asked for at the church service, but it would be probably just me and the vicar singing. Then back to the cars and another slow procession to the cemetery and the committal.

It was then our task to unload the one hundred and fifty or so tributes and lay them out on the ground. These were not just sprays but wreaths of all different shapes and sizes, and various tributes designed specifically to symbolise the deceased. A huge cup and saucer three feet in diameter, a large iron, a dog, a hoover, a purse with money, all flowers of course, an old-fashioned telephone, all crafted in flowers. And, of course, 'DAD', 'GRANDAD', etc., too.

If the grave was one that was being reopened, it could be quite a task. They normally had a marble headstone and curbing, with a number of vases, figurines, and ornaments on them. You had to be very careful to move it all safely aside without damaging it. A later challenge concerning the white marble headstones was when the cemetery staff used strimmers to cut the grass growing round the memorial. The grass would fly onto the grave chippings which would be difficult to clear away, and the strimmed grass could also stain the marble. The family would be extremely upset if they saw this.

A memorable traveller funeral I conducted was from a caravan park near Ninfield. We were to leave for a church in Ore, the other side of Hastings - a distance of ten miles. Trying to keep the hearse, twelve limousines, three flatbed lorries, and thirty cars together was a challenge, and our police escort was essential. We arrived at the church an hour later with no problems so far. After the service we drove to Hastings Cemetery around a mile away. However, there was still one set of traffic lights to negotiate. The police escort ushered the hearse and limousines through the lights but, possibly thinking their job was done, they left us, resulting in the thirty following cars being left behind. Unaware that the cortège had been split up by the lights, we drove into the cemetery, the grave being nearly half a mile from the entrance. However, the following cars did not know where we were going and consequently parked in the car park near the entrance to the cemetery. It took another half an hour for them to walk over the hill and eventually reach us allowing the committal to proceed.

The story of this funeral does not stop there. Through me, they ordered a new marble headstone and curb set. Delivery time was no problem to them; four, five, or even six months was acceptable. I was assured by the mason it would be complete in three months. As I said before, you don't mess with these people. Once you tell them what is going to happen, you're expected to keep to it. But no, the mason delayed the delivery by nearly three months and Christmas was coming. Finally, they arranged to deliver the memorial to the cemetery four days before Christmas. However, unloading the marble, they dropped a piece, breaking it in half. The family who had been told the memorial was being fixed that day had all turned up and they were livid. The mason had to return to London and open their workshop on Saturday. They returned on Sunday, which was Christmas Eve. It had snowed that morning, so the family lit a fire in the cemetery near the grave to keep the family warm. Perhaps surprisingly, but very wisely, no cemetery staff came to protest at this. The memorial was duly fixed, much to the family's and my relief.

I conducted a baby's funeral for the travelling folk from Newhaven with the burial at Hailsham Cemetery. I thought I had allowed plenty of time but they first requested that the baby in the coffin was taken out of the house and placed at the front for people to say their farewells. There were over ninety tributes to be loaded and tied down on the flatbed lorries before we set off on the nineteen-mile journey to the cemetery. We travelled at around twenty miles an hour. Firstly, because that was their tradition, and secondly to prevent the flowers and flower cards from blowing away. I had not expected all of these issues for a baby's funeral. We arrived at the cemetery about an hour later than expected.

For another baby's funeral for the travellers a white horse-drawn hearse was requested. Our normal contact was able to borrow a white hearse owned by a well-known businessman for the occasion, which looked superb.

A really great occasion was a funeral I arranged for a fairground community who were, at that time, parked in a Sussex field. There was a whole ring of traditional showman's caravans and we had to load the willow coffin onto the back of a showman's wagon. When all was ready, a jazz band led us out to the road where we had to wait as the players went back to their cars and drove off first so that they could play us in at the Church. After the service, my wife and I were invited back to the wake. We changed into casual clothes and arrived to enjoy an evening with a barbeque and drinks, seated around a central fire, with the jazz band playing.

6.
MY JOURNEY THROUGH THE INDUSTRY

When I joined Trevor Bennett his main branch, workshops, and garages were in Lewes. He also had a branch in Seaford which consisted of only an arranging room and a chapel of rest. Whilst I arranged the funerals at Lewes, we employed an arranger at the Seaford office. Despite this, I was still responsible for carrying out any removals from the homes or nursing homes there, preparing the coffins required, and conducting their funerals. We were in competition there with Seaford Funeral Services until they also were bought by the new owners of Bennetts Funeral Services after Trevor sold the business prior to his retirement.

Whilst still at Lewes, it was decided to open another branch in Newhaven. The only other funeral director in that town was the Co-op, run by another Mr Bennett, Trevor's cousin. I was to run the Newhaven office whilst we trained two new receptionists. Just as we were closing on our very first day of opening, a couple came in to arrange a funeral! I phoned our administration office in order to book a time and date for the funeral and they assumed I was kidding them. I had to handle the call very carefully to avoid the family realising I was having difficulty being taken seriously. All was finally arranged, and the funeral successfully went ahead. I received a hearty congratulations for starting the business off so well.

Later, R. Butler & Sons were acquired, and I was transferred to work as the funeral director there. It was as busy as Bennetts was when I first joined but again, with large price increases, and the reputation of now being part of a large group, business began to decline. The arranging office and a large garage was sold off and staff made redundant. We moved to a new, much smaller office in another part of Hailsham. This included my first experience of a coffin showroom where clients could be invited to select from a range of styles. The coffins themselves were prepared in a large workshop situated in Seaford, where the vehicles were now also kept.

I was given the opportunity to open another branch of Butler's in Polegate, where we generated a third of our business. However, whilst likely attracting some additional work, the cost of providing premises and further staff would not have been justified at the time. Since then, the population of Polegate has increased considerably and the Co-op Funeral Directors have opened a branch there.

In Hailsham we were in competition with an independent funeral director who, surprisingly, moved into new offices two doors down from our office. Their old office was reopened by a third funeral director under the name of Haines. This company was already well known in Eastbourne and, like us, was also a part of a large national group of funeral directors.

My next career step was to be appointed area manager, based now in Seaford. It was interesting when visiting other branches - which now included Bexhill and Hastings - to see how work routines varied. Some were following traditions well, and in others I found too much idleness. Not an easy time for me. The company also now included a number of branches in Brighton, Hove, Worthing, Littlehampton, and Chichester. Through staff holidays and sicknesses, I had to, on occasion, conduct funerals at these branches, or even be on call at nights should a removal come in. My son helped with removals sometimes. On one occasion, having just helped me on a removal in Hailsham, we went straight on to Hove to do a second removal. My wife also worked as a funeral arranger in a Brighton branch for a few weeks.

As area manager I often had to go to head office in Sutton Coldfield for meetings and learn the latest initiatives, sales techniques, and review customer satisfaction surveys. At one such meeting I managed to be awarded a prize for my ideas and was given a weekend away for my wife and I at the Swan Inn Hotel in Southwold.

It was around this time that I had an accident which changed my career path. I had offered to help carry an empty coffin up from the workshop in Hastings to their Chapel. However, I was not aware of, or warned of, the step I had to walk backwards up. I fell heavily with the coffin, the person on the other end of the coffin adding to the weight as it fell on me. I was subsequently off work with back pain for three months. My doctor advised that I should refrain from heavy lifting.

This occurred at the same time as when Lewes was badly flooded. The Lewes office had to be temporarily shut and the staff laid off. I was offered the position of funeral arranger there, which I accepted. But, for the first time, because of my back injury, I would no longer be on call to do removals. It was a much quieter branch now and I was still able to conduct my own funerals, quite like old times. There was much work to restore everything after the flood. In theory I was part time, but I got busy with building up relations in the community again. One activity I took on was to become secretary to the League of

Friends of the Phoenix Centre which provided a wide range of facilities to the elderly. Another was to start bereavement courses aimed at nurses and care staff. I was also asked to become safety officer for all of the company's Sussex branches, both training staff and inspecting branches to ensure they complied with health and safety regulations. My part-time job became almost a full-time occupation. I built up sufficient trade to take on another funeral arranger who I later trained to conduct funerals before I finally retired.

7.

BURIALS AT SEA

Between 2002 and 2013, 140 people were laid to rest in a watery grave around the UK - many of them former sailors or Royal Navy folk – and, somehow, I became known as the specialist in Sussex for arranging burials at sea. There are only three places around the coast of England that sea burials are permitted to take place, one being off the coast of Eastbourne, another near the Needles, and the third off North Tyneside. The exact position is dictated by the Ministry of Agriculture and Fisheries, some eight miles offshore where there is sufficient depth to avoid the coffin being inadvertently dredged up.

My earlier experiences consisted of using a tugboat based at Newhaven harbour. There were fairly crude facilities for the accompanying family but the crew looked after us well. On one occasion, we went out in a force six wind. I was worried that the coffin would not still be in place when we reached our destination, the boat was pitching about so much. However, the coffin was well tied down. What followed was one of the remarkable experiences of a burial at sea. In the pitching sea, the tug was turned round and round in a tight circle, causing a flat vortex in the water. With waves crashing all about us, into this calm vortex the coffin was slid followed by the floral tributes. The coffin sunk immediately, but to see the flowers just bobbing about was remarkable.

Arranging a burial at sea was a lengthy process, unlikely to take under three weeks but, more commonly, up to four or five weeks. We needed to have a 'Freedom of Infection Certificate,' an 'Out of England Certificate' from the coroner, and permission from the Ministry of Agriculture and Fisheries. Then we had to book the boat. In most recent years we used a craft moored in Sovereign Harbour, Eastbourne; the training vessel of the Maritime Volunteer Service. Then a crew had to be found, and the tides had to be right. And then the weather had to be suitable. Delays could also be at short notice because of the deterioration of the weather. We once had to delay a burial three times.

As usual, our job was to collect the deceased. Usually fairly locally, but occasionally from far away. I have collected from Cromer in Norfolk and from Basildon in Essex. It was on the latter occasion that I achieved the ultimate in providing a superb service. The family telephoned me from Basildon to say they were requesting a burial at sea and the deceased, who was in Basildon Hospital, was ready for collection, so when could we arrange to come up? It just so happened that my crew were collecting someone from Peterborough that morning. It was in the early days of the mobile phone but, fortunately, they did have one so I was able to call them. They were on their way back, and, at that moment, were on the M25 only a couple of miles from the turn off to Basildon. I contacted the family and informed them we would be there in twenty minutes! They were astonished.

Having found out the size of the deceased, we were able to order the coffin. These were specially constructed with a heavy metal plate fixed to the bottom to ensure the coffin sank, as well as large holes drilled around all sides to allow the air out as the coffin sank, preventing the lid blowing off from the pressure.

So, all was arranged, and the day of the funeral would arrive. It would be an early start for us to load the coffin into the hearse at our office and then drive to Sovereign Harbour in Eastbourne to arrive by 8.30am - at least an hour before the family. It would not be very edifying for the family to witness the coffin being loaded onto the boat using a forklift tractor. But, both the weight of the coffin and the height of the boat above the quay necessitated that it was loaded this way. The coffin would then be tied down and the main tribute tied down on the lid.

Up to a dozen family members were able to join us. 'Us' being me, the captain, and four crew. We would sail through the lock gates and off on a journey of around an hour and a half to the designated location, approximately eight miles south of Seaford. The captain and crew, now dressed in their finery, would assemble, ready to assist at the committal. The captain, with all due dignity, would read the committal prayers and the crew would release the coffin into the sea. The family would then cast their floral tributes into the sea.

On the return journey, the crew would always lay on a buffet for the family in the cabin below. I was permitted to helm the boat for part of the return trip which was a great experience. The whole trip would take around five hours.

This was certainly an expensive option for a funeral but that was never a consideration. The deceased would have clearly indicated it was their wish and would have a clear reason for it. On one occasion an ex Royal Marine wished to be buried with many of his fellow comrades who had drowned during the invasion on the Normandy beaches.

Burials at sea were one of the most special events I ever organised. Complicated and time consuming, but they would give the family a huge sense of satisfaction from saying goodbye in this special and meaningful way.

MVS East Sussex 1 is an eighteen-meter Port Tender operated by the Marine Volunteer Service. The coffin was secured on the fore deck whilst being taken out to sea.

8.

FAMILY LIFE

From the beginning, we knew it would be a big family commitment. I was on call three weeks out of four, twenty-four hours a day. Out of normal office hours, all telephone calls came through our home. If I was out, my wife would have to be around to take the call. This was before the age of mobile phones so we used a pager system. It was not always reliable, the Weald being a particularly bad area for reception. If I was out, I would have to find a telephone box to call home.

As mentioned before, calls could come at any time of the day or night. Calls asking us to attend a house to collect a deceased normally meant leaving the house immediately and, often, this seemed to occur around 10pm, just as you had undressed for bed or were even in bed having just turned the light out! If you had friends around, it was 'Excuse me, must be off.'

One of the longest times I was away during what should have been special family time was one Christmas Day. The first call came at 10am and I then had two further calls, eventually getting home at 6pm. On another occasion, my colleague on duty with me informed me he was out for dinner with friends but would still be available. He had hardly sat down to eat when I had to call him out. Shortly after he returned to his friends, I had to call him out again. We completed our work by 10.45pm. I don't know what his hosts must have thought!

Our children, Christopher, Diane, and James soon became used to what, to others, would be bizarre conversations. I would, perhaps, share difficulties encountered or had to plan the day around known commitments - school runs or even music lessons, for example. And, of course, parked outside was my estates car equipped with a stretcher and other paraphernalia needed on a removal. Even a coffin which was on the way somewhere. When I was on call, I always had to ask the children to keep their telephone calls short in case a customer or the coroner called. How annoying for them!

Christopher was able to help me on a number of occasions when the deceased was particularly heavy, requiring more than two people to lift them. There was one unusual time one night when I needed his help to collect a deceased in their coffin from Gatwick Airport. It was a repatriation from Spain and for obvious reasons the airport authorities were keen to have the coffin removed as soon as the plane had arrived. We went right through to the airside; we were obviously not a security risk. Another time, at the funeral of a dear farmer friend, Christopher arranged for a vintage tractor to pull a trailer with the coffin and flowers on board along the A22 and to a local village church for the service and burial. It was a very special feeling to have family so involved in my activities.

James, whilst a young schoolboy, once informed me he was not travelling in my car with a coffin in the back! He later was to become increasingly involved assisting me, as mentioned. Not least due to his being an accomplished organist. When a church was without their own organist, we were responsible for hiring one. So, when he was available, James helped us. He was always keen, and his earnings helped him to pay for flying lessons.

One of James' experiences which caused him, justifiably, to

have a moan was when he played for nearly three quarters of an hour because we were late to the church. The cortège had arrived at a house near Hailsham where the coffin had rested in the house for a couple of days before the funeral. What I had not been told was that they wanted the coffin to be placed on a horse drawn cart and taken on it down the drive. With a six-foot 'gates of heaven' floral arrangement on the back! A distance of two hundred metres. The coffin was then placed into the hearse which was the easy bit. But to tie the six-foot gates of heaven on the roof without breaking it and tying that down was very difficult. The next hold up was that all the mourners had walked down behind the coffin so had to walk back to their cars parked even further away in the field beyond the house. Knowing we had a big cortège; we had asked for a police outrider to enable us to keep the cars together whilst turning on to the A22. However, he only let the hearse and limousines through, thus the following cars had to feed individually onto the main road. Lack of parking space at the village church was the final hinderance. I could only say sorry to James.

He does have a few stories of his own, as well. At one small church, the power of the organ bellows was limited. So, when he was asked to play 'Jerusalem', he had to play the first verse quietly so there was enough power remaining in the bellows to do the crescendo at the end of the second verse. Otherwise, the notes just faded away. In another church organ he once found, it appeared, that a starling had fallen down one of the pipes. Consequently, when he tried to play that note he just got a fluffing noise. At Beddingham Church where he was asked to play, although there was a large organ, when he opened up the console, all he found was a two-octave electric keyboard. Not very inspiring to play for a good send off. At the end of a service for a former serviceman, he was mid-way through a medley of rousing military marches when the daughter of the deceased suddenly appeared in the organ loft and ran across to hug him tightly, thanking him for his playing - all while he continued to play as the cortège moved out of the church.

With my daughter Diane, it is more about the legacy of my dealing with funerals, the experience enabling her to come alongside bereaved friends to help and support them. I was also able to use a company limousine to take Diane to her wedding. The driver was one of my bearers, whilst I was the proud father in the back with her. And, we had someone stay at the house during the ceremony. Not only another bearer, but also someone who had taught her at school. Talk about bringing work home!

For all my children, to talk about death is not a subject they shy away from, and it has helped them in consoling their own friends through bereavement.

My wife was also increasingly involved, and became proficient at arranging funerals. She was able to cover for holidays and sickness in a number of branches in Brighton, Lewes, Seaford, Hailsham, and Bexhill. Quite a challenge at each location, getting to know the different churches and ministers, the local cemeteries and such like, and presenting the options to the family as a knowledgeable and efficient funeral arranger! She commented that often the family seemed to be in a hurry to get everything buttoned up as quickly as possible. What was the rush?

For myself, when I retired, I thought it would be the end of my involvement in funerals. The week before retirement, I had had a chat with an independent funeral director in Uckfield, half joking, saying if I had a funeral to arrange, could he help me. The first week of my retirement, I received two requests to arrange a funeral. Being the local funeral director for three small parishes, and many parishioners knowing me personally, they phoned me at home. I was thus able to carry on arranging and conducting funerals for relatives and friends for another twelve years with this firm, helping with the practical work of preparing the coffin and providing the funeral vehicles and the bearers.

There were two special occasions when my wife and I worked together to line a grave with flowers. The first was for her grandfather who was buried in Crowborough Cemetery. This was in 1989, before my becoming a funeral director, and was my first experience of being closely involved with a funeral. We understood it was a Norfolk tradition to line a grave of a gardener with flowers. As her grandfather had been a gardener for a Norfolk estate, we had decided to continue the tradition. We had enough netting to cover all four sides of the grave and interweaved the netting with a complete covering of flowers before gently securing the netting to the side of the grave. We had warned the gravedigger to ensure there was enough room for the coffin to be lowered without tearing off the flowers. The result was an extremely colourful and very beautiful fitting tribute to a man who had spent his life surrounded by nature. The vivid display of blooms felt like a final embrace, a way of honouring not only his profession but also his love for the land. Seeing the coffin lowered into a grave lined with such care and beauty made the moment feel deeply personal and respectful.

I have a habit that never fails to amuse my family. At every funeral I attend I can't help but mentally score it out of ten. I tend to be quite critical, and I sometimes cringe at the lack of professionalism or attention to detail shown by some funeral directors. For example, the trestles to take the coffin not being placed in the church until the congregation were already waiting for the funeral to start. Once the size of the grave had clearly not been checked and the coffin would not fit. My most regular criticism was for the funeral director and the bearers' casual behaviour waiting to carry the coffin into the service or just wandering out having carried the coffin in. And then, the habit by some companies to use just conductors to lead the proceedings. These were not trained professional funeral directors, had no chance of building a rapport with the client, and didn't even accompany the family home after the service, just – as I often saw - waved to the clients as the limousine drove them off. Their only task seemed to be to usher the family into the service and out again afterwards.

The flower-lined grave

9.

HYMNS AND MUSIC

In the many years of arranging funerals, there has been a big change in the choice of hymns and music. Because of the differing experiences of different generations, what is regarded as socially acceptable alters, and modern technology has also affected this greatly.

When I first started, the older relatives were likely to ask for old hymns, now long forgotten, or simply not known. Many of the older widows had attended Sunday School as children, or had more regularly gone to church, so knew the hymns they wanted such as *'The Old Rugged Cross,' 'O God, Our Help in Ages Past,' and 'The Day Thou Gavest, Lord, has Ended.'* The next generation did not have that experience and were more influenced by what they heard on television. The commonest choice was, and still is, *'The Lord is my Shepherd.'* It may be surprising to know that this hymn was not included in the Church of England's Hymns Ancient and Modern at that time and its popularity led to copies of this hymn being pasted into the hymn books. Other popular choices *are 'Abide with Me,'* again as seen being sung at the FA Cup final and at major rugby matches, and *'Jerusalem,'* as heard being sung with gusto at the last night of the Proms. *'Morning has Broken'* and *'All Things Bright and Beautiful'* - including the *line 'the rushes we gather every day'* – are still common, probably because they are remembered from childhood! Another generation and some of these hymns are surely likely to be forgotten.

The next big change of choice of music came following Princess Diana's funeral which was watched by millions.

Suddenly it became acceptable to have secular music included in the service. Not normally a problem at crematoriums, but for a church service this caused real resistance from the clergy. To have taped music in church? Whatever next! Now, secular music is regularly played at the beginning and end of the service as the coffin is carried in and out.

The music provided by the family was either on tape or, in later years, on CDs. Tapes could be a problem: the actual tape could get all entangled in the player or the wrong section of the tape might end up being played. Trying to run the tape on or wind it back to find the correct music was not realistic to do in a service. Then, when CDs came in, one learnt to always check that the actual CD was in the case. I have had CD cases presented to me for the service only to find, upon opening, there was no CD inside.

Among the choices of music was, for Sussex folk, *'Sussex by the Sea.'* Two beautiful ethereal pieces which I recommended a number of times was *'In Paradisum'* by Gabriel Fauré and *'Over the Rainbow'* sung by Eva Cassidy. Thankfully we never had anyone request *'Smoke Gets in Your Eyes'* at a crematorium service!

I have a special memory of carrying a coffin into a service whilst *'We are the Champions'* by Freddie Mercury was being played at full blast. The deceased was a young lad who was a motorbike enthusiast. It was so appropriate and there was not a dry eye in the place. A common choice, which I really did not like, was *'My Way'* by Frank Sinatra. I suppose it may have summed up the person's character, but I disliked the sentiment.

If recorded music was not requested at the crematorium,

they would employ their own organist. Some were good and led the singing. One I spoke to several times about his playing, but he would not change. The problem was this: if there was only a small congregation he played the hymn very quietly, which he thought was appropriate, but it was so quiet that no one could really follow him. Not useful.

We used a variety of other sources of music. There was a bugler, used at funerals of someone from the Armed Services or representing the Royal British Legion, and we also had bagpipers, solo violinists and even a jazz band. I arranged the funeral of two people who were ballroom dancing champions. For them, the music played was dance music performed by Victor Silvester and his Orchestra.

With the latest trend of using officiants to run a funeral service with no Christian content, modern pop music can make up a lot of the service reflecting much of the life and lifestyle of the deceased. I have yet to experience the congregation actually singing along with one of these songs, but it may well become the norm. All it needs is for a particular piece of music with appropriate words to be used at a funeral of a famous person and it could well become the accepted thing to do.

A final word on the choice of music. I heard a story recently recounted on the radio where the deceased had asked that there should be no service, that his coffin be carried to his place of rest in a tractor and one piece of music played. It was 'Farewell to Stromness' by Peter Maxwell Davies. This is a simple, haunting, and quite beautiful piece of music, full of emotion. What a lovely tune to say goodbye.

10.

THE CORONER CALLS

Trigger warning: descriptions of death

If the cause of death could not be verified by a doctor at a residence, the coroner became involved. The Police would phone the duty Funeral Director for them to collect the deceased and take them to the local hospital, for us that was Eastbourne District General Hospital or The Royal Sussex County Hospital in Brighton. Our company was on call one month in three. They would expect us to attend within half an hour - quite a challenge if you happened to be in bed when they called. The Police were always in attendance at the house and would supervise us. On one occasion, the policeman assured us he had checked the deceased pockets and there was nothing there, but I always checked myself and, on this occasion, found three hundred pounds in his back pocket. What a temptation! It was duly handed over.

There were circumstances where the death occurred outside of a house or other building. For example, as a result of a car crash. Normally an ambulance would have been called to the scene, however, if the person was already confirmed as deceased, the duty funeral director was called to remove the deceased to the hospital mortuary. The sort of thing the coroner may need to establish was if the car crash was caused by a heart attack or the heart attack was the result of the car crash.

We once had to recover two deceased from a field under the gaze of the South Downs. They had both been piloting gliders from a flying club when they collided in mid-air. Fortunately, it was not our job to recover them from the ground, but it involved a two hour wait, standing in solemn stillness as we watched the sun dip behind the hills, a reminder of the fragility of life.

Another case we were urgently requested to attend was a death on the main railway line from Eastbourne to Lewes. It was early morning - a busy time for the trains, but all had been stopped until we had cleared the deceased. Being hit by the train at speed meant the deceased was scattered over several yards. It must have been a very traumatic experience for the train driver. Again, for us, it was an unavoidable task.

One particularly sad case was when a lady died on her pearl wedding anniversary. She and her husband had booked to fly to New York the following day for a holiday. Both her children were already on the way to join them for a celebration later that day. It was before the day of the mobile phone, so they had no idea what had happened until they arrived. During our wait several florists tried to deliver celebratory bouquets of flowers which we were asked to turn away. It was a couple of hours before the family arrived and we had to allow them to say their goodbyes before we were able to take the lady away.

One death of a lady surprised the doctor who had been treating his patient for years with tablets for her heart. It turned out she had never actually taken them: there were rows and rows of unopened tablets on the kitchen shelves.

A rather unpleasant experience of mine was during a call to an address following a sudden death. I was invited to sit down whilst I recorded the details of the deceased. When I said to the family that the chair seemed wet, they said the deceased had died on the chair. He had obviously wet himself on dying; a not unusual occurrence. But most unpleasant to sit in it!

More unpleasant were suicides. If they had shot themselves, it could be an extremely unpleasant task to lift the deceased onto a stretcher ready to load in the waiting removal vehicle. How can you get used to it, you might wonder? There was no option not to: it is part of the responsibilities one takes on as a funeral director and training and experience enabled you to take appropriate action. If I was accompanied by someone inexperienced with this, I would go in first and do my best to cover the deceased up before we began the removal procedure. A hanging was horrible. If someone had committed suicide with exhaust fumes from their car, the most unpleasant aspect to me was the smell.

Finally, there was Beachy Head with its six-hundred-foot cliffs. People came from all over the country with its reputation as a site where people could end their lives. There were up to two dozen suicides a year. The Coastguard and the Police would be in attendance at each one. We would await the body being recovered and brought up the cliffs by the coastguard team and we would then take the deceased to Eastbourne Hospital, waiting outside the ambulance entrance for a doctor to come out to confirm the death. We were told on more than one occasion by ambulance drivers that we couldn't park there. They did not see the body bag in the back of the car and realised why we had to wait there. From here we would then go to the mortuary, undress the deceased, and place them into the refrigerator.

It would be understandable curiosity if you were wondering what job I found most unpleasant. I won't go into detail but, briefly, removing a deceased who had been deceased for a number of days or even weeks - the neighbour, who lived below, had reported stains coming through the ceiling. A close second would be removing someone who had been killed in a fire.

Following removal to the hospital, a post-mortem would be carried out to establish the cause of death. Once this was determined, an inquest was opened to formally confirm the identity of the deceased and report the death. One often reads in the news that an inquest has been opened and adjourned. This essentially allows the deceased to be released for burial or cremation. Delays here could cause families, wishing to get a funeral date fixed, a lot of anguish. But, by experience, we knew we dare not hint at a date so as to avoid giving families false expectations.

How were these jobs when compared with the normal day to day funeral business? As I explained before, with training, and thorough experience, I knew what procedures we needed to follow. Dealing with day-to-day funerals required far more personal commitment and attention to detail, though, as you were dealing face to face with the bereaved with all their emotions.

A big challenge could occur if the family wished to see the deceased after they had had a postmortem. The mortuary procedure involved cutting open the cranium to inspect the brain. The cranium would be closed and the skin sewn back, but when you were preparing the deceased for the family to see, you had to ensure the cranium had not shifted lest you saw a ridge across the forehead. The chest is also cut open to check the organs and, likewise, the skin is sewn back afterwards. So, another task for us to ensure none of this was apparent.

And what helped? I got on very well with the coroner's officer who was a fellow bee keeper and was also the auctioneer at the annual Bee Fair. So, through my hobby I got to know and work with him very well.

11.

THE QUESTION ABOUT ASHES

Ashes - what to do with them? This, I noticed, was a frequently unanswered question. The decision of burial or cremation may have been settled long ago, but thoughts on what to do with the ashes had often not been decided upon or had even been considered. Sometimes families may have not even known that, following a cremation, there were ashes. Frequently there were different views from within a family.

There are so many options to choose from and it was our job to explain them, if the family had yet to decide. They can be scattered at the crematorium, buried at a crematorium or cemetery with, possibly, a grave marker or tablet, they can be taken for later burial in a church yard - perhaps in an existing grave or an ashes plot, or buried or scattered in the garden or in the countryside. A relatively new option is to have the ashes in a managed woodland burial site with the option of having the space marked with a wooden plaque or rustic stone.

A further choice made by some was to have the ashes scattered at sea. From the beach, from a pier or from a boat. A donation to the Royal National Lifeboat Institution was often made following a request for their help. Once, there was a request to have the ashes sent up in a rocket from Firle Beacon at the top of the South Downs.

The next problem for the funeral director was the timing of when the decision was made. If the family knew before the funeral was arranged, no problem. Hopefully, from the funeral director's point of view, they would decide on the arrangement, but often they would say they had to consult with the rest of the family. The longer the delay in deciding, the more difficult that decision became. One of the chief reasons for this was one's emotions change over the period of grief. What are at first such strong emotions become more bearable over time. The decision to do something becomes one of tying up the loose ends. Or maybe, after a protracted period of time, the family would just forget.

We were asked to keep the ashes at our office until a decision was made, but that could turn into months, if not years! The longer the delay, the more likely the family would say they would have to consult with the rest of the family. Then there were occasions we found the family had moved away and there was no forwarding address. You could finish up with dozens of ashes containers on the shelf. Ultimately, after due warning, the ashes were returned to the crematorium for scattering.

There was one nerve-wracking occasion I had when the family was due to collect the ashes, but I could not find them among our collection of containers. I looked and looked. What would I say to the family? They would likely be so cross. Being on some low shelving I finally got down on my knees for a closer inspection. There they were. The surname had been written by the crematorium on the line below where they should have been written. That was a close call.

When I first got involved with Newhaven Cemetery, they had no facilities for the burial of ashes so our company sponsored the construction of an area where ashes could be buried and memorial tablets placed. However, a problem later arose when the partner of the already buried person died. The

Council would not allow a second person to be buried in the same plot. No chance of saying 'together again.' They would, instead, be buried several plots away. Some big arguments arose but the council did not change their mind. I can only hope that, since my retirement, they have changed this decision which caused real distress for families.

As with church graveyards, ashes plots in churchyards are also becoming restricted. One local church I know of has stated that, when the existing ashes plots are filled, another area for ashes will not be allocated. Perhaps understandable in a nearly full town churchyard, but in a rural churchyard, with adequate space, this seems rather uncompassionate. So, where will people have the ashes placed where they can have some sort of memorial - normally taking the form of a small tablet. There are opportunities for a private company to provide spaces and who are surely likely to offer additional ways of marking the grave. A choice of different styles of tablets, vases or figurines surrounded by well-kept gardens. All at an additional charge.

A new option for the storing of cremated remains has recently been offered by way of niches contained in newly constructed stone burial chambers or mounds. Taking the idea from prehistoric barrows, new structures across the UK - including Cambridgeshire and Shropshire, have been designed and built containing niches specifically to take ashes urns. There are different size niches from single spaces to large niches which will take multiple caskets with spaces that can be leased for a period of time from a year up to ninety-nine years. The barrows have been beautifully crafted, and the niches can be further personalised by having carved stone coverings, hand painted doors, or stained-glass windows. Likely an expensive option, but a beautiful and peaceful resting place for cremated ashes, knowing that the whole structure will be carefully looked after for many years to come. They are described not as a place of sorrow or sadness, but rather a gallery of life, memories, and happiness. I'd recommend visiting a barrow open day simply to take in the extraordinary architecture and quiet stillness.

I believe marking the end of a life in a meaningful way, whatever that is, is so important. One can look back on where the ashes were placed with a sense of satisfaction and peace that you have said and completed a proper goodbye.

Credit: Paul Gillett

Woodvale Crematoriam, Brighton. The chapels were build in 1856 and converted to a crematoriam in 1930. It was the first crematoriam to be established in Sussex.

Wealdon Crematoriam near Horum was opened in 2019.

12.
THE DAWN OF THE FUNERAL GROUP

When I first joined Bennet Funeral Services in Lewes, the majority of funeral directors were small independent companies with perhaps two or three branches. Around five years after I joined, Trevor Bennet decided to retire and sold to a company based in the North. It was run by two young men who had great aspirations to build a large group which would result in lower operating costs and more profits. However, their inexperience caused real problems. They tended to micromanage everything - very frustrating to experienced funeral directors. And charges went up to cover the cost incurred by the loans needed to buy the company in the first place.

Another problem was that the remaining independent funeral directors made great play of us now being a large national company. This had a detrimental effect on the numbers of funerals we did, exacerbated by the opening of a second funeral director in Lewes. The only large group which didn't suffer was the Co-operative funeral company probably due to their presence across the country being recognised for many years.

The company was then taken over by an American group, SCI. Worse publicity followed. People did not want to be buried by an American. Prices were hiked again and more business lost. Over a period of five years business at Lewes we went from 350 funerals a year to 80. The situation was remedied by a management buy-out in 2002, when the UK funeral services market was valued at around £800m. The directors were experienced funeral directors who managed to raise standards and restore the company's reputation, launching the Dignity brand. They are now one of the leading nationally known funeral directors.

One of the companies absorbed into the Dignity group was Kenyons. One of Kenyons' divisions was Kenyons Emergency Services who specialised in disaster management across the world. This included natural disasters, the results of terrorist attacks, and major transportation incidents involving multiple deaths. The importance of collecting personal effects together for the remaining family in the aftermath of a mass fatality incident cannot be understated, and Kenyons had supplies and equipment strategically located in warehouses around the world. They had their own expert staff and through Dignity had access to additional staff to help on occasions. This included my staff on a couple of occasions, hence the inclusion of Kenyons in this book. To support families to come to terms with the trauma of their experience was something I believe I was able to help with.

I will mention three incidents to give you an example of the sort of situations in which Kenyons were involved. In 1987 the Herald of Free Enterprise, a roll-on/roll-off ferry, capsized minutes after leaving the Belgian port of Zeebrugge. The ship had left the harbour with her bow doors open causing the decks to flood and the ferry to capsize, killing 193 passengers. The difficulty of removing the deceased was immense as, with the ship lying on its side, the men had to walk on the walls and then the doors which were now lying flat.

There were two major incidents in the following year. One, a disaster on the Piper Alpha oil rig when it exploded killing 165 men. The other, the blowing up by terrorists of Pan Am Flight 103 over Lockerbie. The Boeing 747 was on a flight from London Heathrow to New York. All two hundred and fifty-nine passengers were killed plus eleven residents living in Lockerbie. The task of recovering both persons and their effects must have been daunting and traumatic, even for experienced staff. The mortuary facilities initially provided were in a basement, creating the handicap of having to carry the deceased up and down the stairs. The mortuary was later transferred to a local ice rink which had been covered over. The importance of having a body for the family to grieve over is paramount and here was an occasion where body parts had to be assembled back together. Not an easy or pleasant job.

Another matter pertaining to funerals was the introduction by funeral groups of pre-paid funerals. Initially, the task of arranging these with a client was done by 'experienced' salesman. Unfortunately, ones not in the funeral industry! For example, mistakes were made charging for obituaries at local newspaper prices whereas the client wanted an allowance for an insert in *The Times* newspaper, which was four or five times more expensive. Another mistake made was calculating mileage. They may know the distance and the mileage rate but forgot there was the return journey to add. We had one arranged where the deceased was to be taken from Lewes to Carlisle where only one way of the journey was allowed for. A very expensive mistake which we became liable for. Fortunately, this arrangement did not last too long, and we were once again able to organise these pre-paid funerals ourselves. Pre-paid funerals were originally only advertised in branches. It was considered inappropriate to advertise them in television adverts and in national newspapers and consequently it wasn't until 1998 that Dignity ran the first ever funeral plan TV advert with Age Concern.

Funeral services were originally provided by the local builder or carpenter. Such companies still exist in Balcombe and Hartfield. When I joined Trevor Bennett, they were the only funeral director in Lewes. In Uckfield there were three independent companies. When one owner retired, he sold to one of the others in Uckfield, although they still trade under their old name. They have since been joined by the Co-op funeral services. Four companies serving a population of 15,000. In the nearby town of Heathfield, with a population of only 7,600 residents, there are five funeral directors offering their services! Obviously, they cover the surrounding areas too, but it shows the potential business opportunities. It also shows there are still opportunities for small independent funeral directors to effectively compete with the larger groups through being more flexible and personal.

The advantage of belonging to a group of companies was not only sharing funeral vehicles. Our company also had a minibus available for local branches to take residents of nursing homes out for trips. A benefit much appreciated by the owners of the nursing home and it helped promote good relations between us. Sometimes the trip was purely an outing around the countryside, sometimes to a café or pub for lunch or tea. One nursing home in Hailsham requested several times a trip to Rye. And, a favourite of all: a trip to Drusillas Park where I helped to push some of the residents around in wheelchairs. The zoo was interesting for the first couple of times but, after the tenth time, somewhat boring. We did lose a resident there once. We did not realise until we all got back into the minibus. Fortunately, I had been taking photos on an instant camera. We searched through them and found when she was last seen. We went back in and found that she had peeled off at the restaurant and was in the process of ordering soup.

Another advantage of belonging to a national group of funeral directors came when arranging long distance funerals. There was always a local contact who could help with information, vehicles, or even removals.

The small independent director still has one big advantage over the large groups, though. At Bennetts, I was the person who took the phone call or met the family when they came into the office. I was the person who called at the house to collect the deceased. It was I who arranged the funeral in our office or at their home. And it was I who conducted the funeral, caring for the family from beginning to the end. With a large group, in nearly every instance, this would involve a different person at each stage so little chance of the family building up a real relationship with the company. As I mentioned in chapter 8, there are some companies who use a funeral conductor instead of a fully qualified funeral director at the actual funeral service. He would not have the technical knowledge to assist the family through all aspects of options and procedures relating to a funeral. That was not the personal service which I strived to achieve.

Another change during my time in the industry was the increasing use of lady funeral directors. There was one company which was actually created to appeal to potential clients through offering this service - The Caring Lady Funeral Director. And they went on to do very well.

Larger companies have now become involved in the crematorium business, too. They were to take over existing businesses or have built brand new crematoriums providing modern chapels, well laid out grounds, and large car parking facilities. Lack of parking space had become a real problem for many of the older crematoriums. These companies are keen to offer or exploit ever further options of memorialising the deceased. They seem to bristle with options for buying a seat, plaques, tablets, rose bushes, trees, and engraved markers. Commemorating the deceased has become big business.

There is a strong case to be made that the introduction of competition in this area has been beneficial. In Brighton, there are two crematoriums next door to each other. One is run by the local council, the other by a national company. They both bend over backwards to provide a good service and work well with the funeral director. Unfortunately, in certain other council-run crematoriums, it seemed they felt the funeral director was there for the crematorium's benefit. The other crematoriums which we used were in Eastbourne, Hastings, Tunbridge Wells, Crawley, and Worthing. In Tunbridge Wells their facilities were limited and could be awkward in shepherding a family through the chapel. There has been the construction of a new crematorium near Horam by a national company with modern facilities and ample parking now, and this company has attracted a lot of business.

Finally, the provision of woodland burial cemeteries is, as I mentioned before, a relatively new option. The two municipal cemeteries I knew who created such spaces used completely open ground, but their policy was to plant a tree or trees round the grave. The more rural ones were in existing woodlands. The first one I visited was on the outskirts of Norwich, a really beautiful, established woodland. The charge for this option is likely to be much higher than a traditional cemetery. If the object is to purely benefit nature, I believe a donation to a wildlife charity is far more helpful. However, a natural woodland setting is appealing.

13.

DEATH AND RITUALS OVER THE CENTURIES

Going back centuries, death in many families was often caused by disease, poverty, and famine. The burial of the dead in most circumstances would be a simple, and very much a local, affair.

In the 16th century, it was common for a family to have eight to ten children, hoping that some would survive to help the family on the farm or in whatever trade they followed. Twelve percent of children died in their first year. And death in childbirth was not uncommon, with only an untrained local lady likely to be called along to help with the birth. By the eighteenth century the average number of children in a family was five, but still one in five did not make their fifth birthday. The average age of death of an adult then was thirty-four years for a man and forty-two years for a woman.

In the Middle Ages, following the death of someone in the family, the majority of families would follow the simplest rituals. The body would be washed, dressed in a shroud, and laid out in the home. A task likely to be done, again, by a local woman used to such rituals. The house would be open to the local community to come in to pay their respects. The parish priest would be asked to read the last rites. The 'Order for the Burial of the Dead' was laid out by the Act of Uniformity of Common Prayer in 1559 (and is still in use today). The introduction to the Order for the Burial of the dead reads:

'Here is it to be noted, that the Office ensuing is not to be used for any that die unbaptised, or excommunicated, or has laid violent hands on themselves.'

Hence the need for infants to be baptised as soon as possible, as the death of an infant was not uncommon in the 16th and 17th Centuries.

It goes on to say:

'The Priest and Clerks, meeting the Corpse at the entrants of the Church-yard, and going before it, either into the Church, or towards the Grave, shall say or sing:

'I am the resurrection and the life, saith the Lord; he that believeth in me, though he were dead, yet shall he live; and whosoever liveth and believeth in me shall never die.'

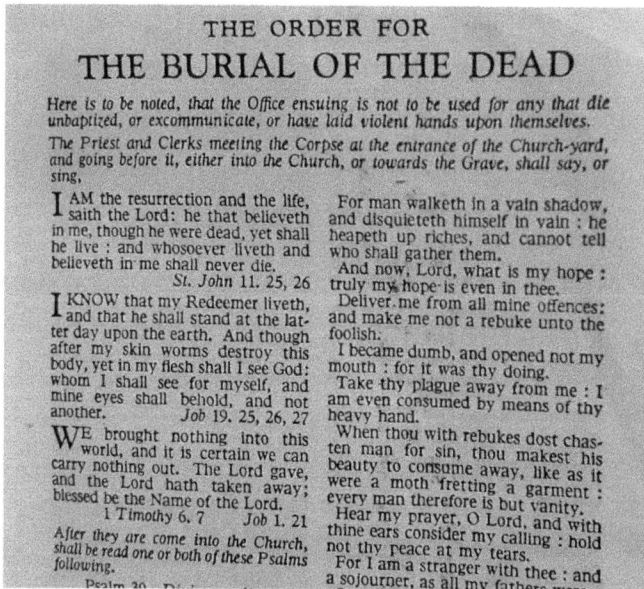

THE ORDER FOR
THE BURIAL OF THE DEAD

Here is to be noted, that the Office ensuing is not to be used for any that die unbaptized, or excommunicate, or have laid violent hands upon themselves.

The Priest and Clerks meeting the Corpse at the entrance of the Church-yard, and going before it, either into the Church, or towards the Grave, shall say, or sing,

I AM the resurrection and the life, saith the Lord: he that believeth in me, though he were dead, yet shall he live : and whosoever liveth and believeth in me shall never die.
St. John 11. 25, 26

I KNOW that my Redeemer liveth, and that he shall stand at the latter day upon the earth. And though after my skin worms destroy this body, yet in my flesh shall I see God: whom I shall see for myself, and mine eyes shall behold, and not another. *Job 19. 25, 26, 27*

WE brought nothing into this world, and it is certain we can carry nothing out. The Lord gave, and the Lord hath taken away; blessed be the Name of the Lord.
1 Timothy 6. 7   Job 1. 21

After they are come into the Church, shall be read one or both of these Psalms following.

Psalm 39.

For man walketh in a vain shadow, and disquieteth himself in vain : he heapeth up riches, and cannot tell who shall gather them.

And now, Lord, what is my hope : truly my hope is even in thee.

Deliver me from all mine offences: and make me not a rebuke unto the foolish.

I became dumb, and opened not my mouth : for it was thy doing.

Take thy plague away from me : I am even consumed by means of thy heavy hand.

When thou with rebukes dost chasten man for sin, thou makest his beauty to consume away, like as it were a moth fretting a garment : every man therefore is but vanity.

Hear my prayer, O Lord, and with thine ears consider my calling : hold not thy peace at my tears.

For I am a stranger with thee : and a sojourner, as all my fathers were.

The 1559 Order of Service for Burial, taken from the Book of Common Prayer.

It is quite astonishing that the service, which was to become so well known to me, was written in 1549 and is still said at nearly every Church of England burial. Note, also, it uses the word 'corpse' and not 'coffin,' as one would expect in this day and age. But it could be because the poor could not afford a coffin, so were buried in a shroud.

In earlier centuries, the minister would likely have a position of authority over the community. He would be a man of letters and likely live in a very substantial house compared with the rest of the community. This was partly because of the inheritance rules of this country: the eldest son from a wealthy family or the aristocracy would inherit the property and title. The next son could be bought a commission in the army, and the third son bought a living as a vicar. Hence, the vast size of many traditional vicarages.

In mediaeval times, the word 'undertaker' was used vaguely for anyone undertaking a task involving the disposal of the dead. Typically, they were the local builder or carpenter who had the skill to make a coffin. If they had a horse and cart, they could also transport the coffin to the church but for many families, family and friends would carry the coffin to the local church. That's if they could afford a coffin, otherwise they were simply wrapped in a shroud. In the country, they could simply be buried in the ground about them. As a profession, undertakers became increasingly involved in every aspect of the care of the deceased and the burial arrangements. And, later, cremations which started to get popular in the 1950s. A common term used to describe such firms up to that time was 'Undertakers and Funeral Furnishers.' However, in 1935, the British Undertakers Association - first formed in 1905, changed their name to the National Association of Funeral Directors. However, the title of Funeral Directors was not taken up for some while after. Records of companies, including R. Butler & Sons, where I worked, still used the term Undertakers and Funeral Furnishers as recently as 1947.

DR. TO

G. C. TANNER & SONS

Undertakers & Funeral Furnishers

CREMATIONS ARRANGED

FUNERALS CONDUCTED BY MOTOR HEARSE OR RAIL TO ALL PARTS

108 LONDON ROAD, SOUTHEND-ON-SEA.

Mr Wager   April 22nd/94 7

Dear Sir,

       Re enquiry of Death Certificate. I am afraid
you will have to get in touch with Mr. Waring of
Elma Lodge, Weir Pond Road, Rochford, Essex.
As the Disposal Certificate is kept by the Cemetery
Authorities. The Registrar will forward you a copy
for a small fee:

       I remain,

               Yours Truly

               G. C. Tanner

Telephone—2384 SOUTHEND

DR. TO

G. C. TANNER & SONS
Undertakers & Funeral Furnishers
CREMATIONS ARRANGED

FUNERALS CONDUCTED BY MOTOR HEARSE OR RAIL TO ALL PARTS
108 LONDON ROAD, SOUTHEND-ON-SEA.

Mr Wager   April 17th 1947

For Funeral & Interment of the late

To

   Supplying One Polished Elm Coffin fitted with Nickel
Silver Handles, Ornaments & Mounted Engraved Name Plate
Lined with Embossed, Ruffles & Side Sheets.
Coffining body with Assistance & Removing from the
Southend Municipal Hospital to Private Mortuary
Fees for Interment & Minister at Woodgrange Park
Conveyance by Motor Hearse & I Mourning Coach from
Southend to Woodgrange Park Cemetery.
Undertakers Personal Attendance & Conducting

	£	s	d
	32	0	0
Grave Fees	9	4	0
Total	£41	4	0

Settled By Cheque
With Many Thanks
April 17th 1947.
G. C. Tanner.

The terminology used in the invoice would certainly not be used today.

    Reading such documents also reveals some rather quaint descriptions of the services these companies offered in the 1940s. *'Funerals conducted by motor hearse or rail to all parts.'* By rail? How was that achieved? Well, it was well before Beeching's savage cuts to the railway network so there was still the facility of reaching many small villages in the country. *'Conveyance by motor hearse and motor mourning coach.'* No longer horse drawn, then. And when did the mourning coach become known as a limousine?

'Cremations and temporary sanitation.' Cremations were only just becoming common, so their mention in company headed paper must have been used to impress the use of these 'modern' facilities. Certainly, one would not use the term 'temporary sanitation' to advertise your services today.

Cremations only became available in Sussex in the 1930s. The local undertakers quickly altered their correspondance to advertise this 'modern' facility.

For many years coffins were handcrafted using oak or elm, elm being particularly resistant to rot. Hence the use of elm in bridge supports. This has now changed. First, because crematoriums required more easily combustible wood, and secondly, Dutch elm disease necessitated another wood be used. Finally, plywood or MDF started to be used with a covering of foil, veneer, or cloth. More recently, the use of cardboard, wicker, and bamboo has become common.

A major influence on the rituals associated with a funeral in Britain was the death of Queen Victoria's husband, Prince Albert. The queen's profound and prolonged period of mourning was to influence all aspects of the rituals associated with a death and these have lasted through to modern times: ornate coffins, formal processions leading to the service held in church, and elaborate memorials. Before the beginning of the 19th century there was still disparity between the aristocracy and the majority of the population, so funeral rituals similarly contrasted. It was the effect of so many people being killed during the First and Second World Wars that made the commemoration of the deceased a more formal and recognised ritual.

Changes have also occurred in Churchyards. Many parish churches are hundreds of years old and would have had many people buried in their churchyard over that time, in mostly unmarked graves. The ground was, therefore, able to be used again and again over the centuries. Only the wealthy were likely to be able to afford a gravestone. In Laughton, it was not unusual when digging a grave to find bones, which the gravedigger quickly buried out of sight. However, these days, it is most unusual not to have a grave marked with a memorial stone. Hence, churchyards have run out of space and have had to create new extensions or direct the family to the local cemetery.

Even now, I believe, much of the choice of styles of coffin

offered are Victorian in design. Other customs that were to be introduced in Victorian times were in the family home: curtains were closed, the clocks stopped, mirrors covered, and family photographs turned down. And prayers at the funeral service used by Church of England vicars are still frequently taken straight from the *Common Book of Prayer*, written in 1549.

There has been a quite recent change to funeral practices in the Roman Catholic faith that is interesting to mention. Until 1963, burials were the only arrangement permitted if the deceased was a Catholic. It was then that the Vatican first permitted cremation as long as it did not suggest a denial of faith about resurrection. In my early days as funeral director - the mid-1980s, it was still fairly uncommon to arrange a cremation for a Catholic.

In the 1980s the Humanist Society was really the only organisation to use if a non-religious service was requested. However, they had their own set of beliefs, and the first part of the service was often taken up by explaining these. With no hymns being sung, sadly there was little opportunity for the congregation to be involved in the service.

It was really the beginning of the 21st century that 'officiants' began to be more regularly used. Of no religious or organisational affiliation, these persons operate independently. As such, they were chosen through recommendations from previous funerals they had conducted, and many became very proficient, personable, and successful. So much so that, as I understand it, nearly half of all cremation services are led by one today. Having recently experienced both types of service in the same week I can understand why many now choose this form of service. The funeral of a young man led by an officiant was incredibly personal and emotional and had everyone participating. No hymns but plenty of modern music, expressing the life of the young man to the congregation. The other, a classic Church of England service with traditional language but little said concerning the individual by the minister. It felt remote. All due dignity but lacking in empathy.

Another tradition that has changed is the wearing of hats by ladies in church. Once always worn but now rarely seen, except in strict Baptist churches. In crematoriums, even less so. I have even seen ladies remove their hats prior to coming into a crematorium service. They must have felt out of place with them on.

There are two traditions I would like to mention which I have experienced abroad and found particularly interesting. Whilst attending a funeral in Canada, the evening before the funeral, family and friends gathered in a large, well decorated room at the undertakers. There was a buffet laid out and drinks served. At the back of the room was an open coffin with the deceased lying there all nicely dressed. Everyone was chatting and sharing experiences and going up to the coffin to perhaps share further their experiences and to say their goodbyes. After an hour, a minister present ended the evening with prayers. The funeral the following day was a traditional Roman Catholic Service. At another Roman Catholic Service, this time in France, as part of the service ritual, everyone in the congregation went up to the coffin and sprinkled holy water on the coffin.

Since I retired, a new dimension has come into funeral services. Pictures and videos can be displayed on large screens to show aspects of the deceased's life. And, through the marvels of the internet, the service can be watched by people throughout the world. Where families are dispersed, it must be a comfort to join the service if they are unable to actually travel to the service.

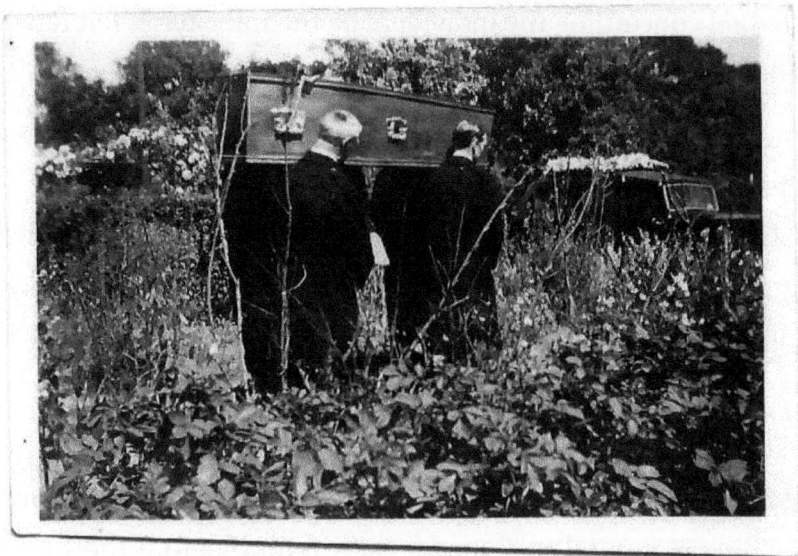

A family funeral from the early 1940s. Nothing has changed much in nearly 100 years.

14.
THE ADVENT OF THE 'UNATTENDED' FUNERAL

Over the years I did arrange a limited number of funerals where no one attended, either as an expressed wish or because the family simply could not be bothered. We would still use our hearse and carry the coffin into the crematorium chapel in a dignified manner. I would then stay, say the committal prayer, and press the button to close the curtains around the coffin.

Today, an 'Unattended Funeral' is advertised widely, initially by national companies specialising in this. The service is now offered by most funeral directors because of the competition for this part of the business and because of the greater awareness of this cheaper option.

The choice of an unattended cremation has been encouraged by phrases such as these:

'Our direct cremation gives you the freedom to have a truly personal celebration of life.' Really?

'It is quickly becoming one of the most popular funeral options.' True - by 2024 they make up over 20% of all funerals

'You don't want to spend thousands on something formal and impersonal.'

'All fees included for an unattended cremation at our trusted partner crematoriums.'

'You don't want the family going through an upsetting service at the crematorium.' Are they saying it does away with the pain of mourning?

And the final reason given: 'The deceased would not have wanted a traditional funeral.'

All the advertisements emphasise the high degree of care, dignity, and attention they give to each funeral and the responses from clients would seem to bear this out. This should always have been the endeavour of a funeral director. The crematorium attendant has become a 'Cremation Experience Associate' to help reassure the family that a dignified funeral will still be carried out, even without the family present. Reputation is everything. As with any funeral, any slip up or sloppiness is likely to be met by extreme anger, this being a common emotion of bereavement. Hence the need to reassure the client with these assurances. As I write, this feeling of trust is being stretched by the news that police have found a funeral director has been storing up bodies before having them cremated. This will likely cause a real hit on the choice of this type of funeral for some time.

There are a number of stipulations regarding the choice of an unattended funeral. The family cannot ever attend the funeral, nor can they decide which crematorium is used or what time it would be carried out. Some companies stipulate that arrangements can only be made in their offices - or by telephone - during working hours. Calling at a private residence is extra, as is the cost of an oversize coffin; unfortunately, more relevant in recent times. And, obviously, no hearse is used, just a suitable vehicle transferring the coffin or coffins to the designated crematorium. In one case I know of, a person was taken from Brighton to near Southampton for the cremation, this being their 'designated' crematorium and likely to be owned by the company organising the funeral. All to minimise costs to the company and ultimately the cost to the customer.

The cost of a funeral has escalated considerably over the last thirty years. Providing a twenty-four-hour service, three hundred and sixty-five days a year, is obviously expensive. The premises would have to include an arranging room, an administrative office, a workshop, a mortuary, and storage for coffins. Then there are the vehicles required: hearses, limousines, removal vehicles, and a company car for the funeral director to do his visits, all to be kept in tip top condition and garaged. The cost of having immaculate hearses and limousines is high considering how often they are used each week. Here is a major advantage of larger funeral groups as they can ensure the different branches work together to maximise the use of these vehicles.

And then there are the additional costs of the ever-wider range of options to enhance the funeral experience: a wider choice of coffins with a big difference in their costs, expensive obituary notices, extravagant floral arrangements, and printed orders of service can well add several hundred pounds to the cost. There is a huge range of memorialisation options offered. This particularly applies to ashes: at crematoriums, there are entries into memorial books, wall tablets, plinths, stone tablets, planting of rose bushes, shrubs, and trees. Finally, there is the option of choosing from a variety of ashes caskets or even encapsulation of ashes.

The final reason for the increase in the cost of a funeral is that the cost of acquiring a funeral director to add to the company's portfolio has to be financed. I had an unfortunate experience following one of these takeovers when we were told to increase our charges by £300 per funeral. I had to explain our increased cost to a customer who had only arranged a funeral with us the month before. He decided to go elsewhere.

My views on this? The option of not attending a funeral was always there. The coffin need only be simple. You don't need to choose a limousine. Some crematoriums offer a reduced price if the funeral is before 10am, a little used time slot for the crematorium. I would be concerned if people went direct to a national company specialising in this service unless the company were also open about the real benefits of having an attended funeral. There is no way around grief, only through it. Saying your goodbye with your family and friends supporting you is hugely beneficial. Personalising that funeral may add to the cost but helps express special memories or significant events in the person's life and such events will be remembered for many years after.

I have one further thought on such funerals. A death of a close relative or friend can be a time of indescribable pain and loss, a time of stunned bewilderment. With this in mind, an attended funeral can be a special time of support and sharing with other members of the family and of friends in attendance, as well as giving them the opportunity to express their grief and a chance to say goodbye. With unattended funerals this opportunity is lost. Perhaps a memorial get-together later can be of help, but everyone's feelings and grief have moved on so this will influence their experience of this occasion. Where the expense of a full funeral could be of real concern to a family, this new option could be of considerable relief though. And, of course, personal circumstances, including the wish of the deceased, can make this option the right decision.

I have myself attended a funeral as a mourner to find that the cremation has already taken place. There was no coffin there, and I felt sad not to have a chance to say a more personal farewell. A memorial service at a later date has a different purpose, and the sense of grief has already moved on.

So, with the ever-rising cost of living and the competition among funeral directors for business, the option of a cheaper unattended funeral is likely to become more popular and also more socially acceptable. It will be interesting to see if the funeral trade will start to offer a follow up service in some form to help the family complete their goodbyes. Indeed, a 'Goodbye Service' might be more appropriate than a Thanksgiving Service. No false pleasantries, just an opportunity to simply express sorrows. Perhaps a printed format could be devised for people to follow with suggested readings or prayers which the family can select.

As the funeral trade has increased the options of spending more money on personalised coffins, they will surely come up with services after an unattended funeral has taken place. Perhaps an even greater emphasis around the person's ashes and their final disposal. Indeed, there is already a company offering to have ashes to be placed in newly built barrows, at a cost. Another company is offering the scattering of ashes by drone "over beautiful and memorable locations across the UK over land or sea." Crematoria offer a wide range of ways of memorialising a person's ashes which, in the past, the family could come to on occasions. If the families have no contact with the crematorium, where do the ashes go? Local churchyards often have little space and even less optional of memorialisation. So, what can the family do to help process their grief and have a place to visit and remember them? Something quite important when deciding on an unattended funeral.

Finally, there is a new option whereby one remembers their loved one with the help of AI powered technology. Chatbot avatars of people can be developed to build a portfolio of the deceased so, ultimately, one can carry on a conversation with the deceased. One will never need to say goodbye! Is this an attempt to eliminate grief as an emotion, though? There must be a danger in distracting ourselves and taking us away from our legitimate, honest experience of grief and loss.

APPENDIX
FAVOURITE PRAYERS AND READINGS

Prayers are quite easy to list as services often repeated them, read from the *Common Book of Prayer*. I have heard many modern contemporary prayers, but they are not so easy to remember.

The first prayer summarises the end of a busy day or even a busy life, and it's time to take a rest:

O Lord, support us all the day long of this troublous life, until the shades lengthen and the evening comes, the busy world is hushed, the fever of life is over and our work is done; then Lord, in thy mercy, grant us a safe lodging, a holy rest, and peace at the last, through Jesus Christ our lord, Amen.

The second is just a lovely blessing:

Unto God's gracious mercy and protection, we commit thee. The Lord bless thee and keep thee. The Lord make his face shine upon thee, and be gracious unto thee. The Lord lift up his countenance upon thee, and give thee peace, both now and evermore. Amen.

Now two readings which help express our loss whilst also acknowledging the special times we have shared with the person who has died. The first was written by David Harkins. Difficult to fully take on in the early stages of grief but a nice encouragement to remember him in a positive way:

You can shed tears that he has gone, or you can smile because he has lived. You can close your eyes and see all that he has left. Your heart can be empty because you can't see him or you can be full of love that you shared. You can turn your back on tomorrow because of yesterday. You can remember that he has gone or you can cherish his memory and let it live on. You can cry and close your mind, be empty and turn your back or you can do what he would want: smile, open your eyes, love and go on.

The second is a real tear-jerker, and really expresses the loss one can feel and the suddenness of death. It was written by Johanne Turner, who gave her permission for it to be reproduced here:

If I'd known the last hug we had, would be the last we'd ever have, I'd hug you harder.

If I'd known that the last joke you told me, would be the last you'd ever tell me, I'd have laughed longer.

If I'd known that the last fire we sat around, would be the last we ever sat around, I'd have stayed until the embers burned black.

If I'd known that the last time we texted into the night, would be the last message we'd ever send, I'd have texted 'till dawn.

If I'd known that the last time we talked about writing a two man show, would leave me as a one man show, I'd stay until we'd written it.

If I'd known that the fire, the jokes, the messages, the friendship would soon be precious memories, then I wish I'd hugged you harder.

There is a third reading which is often used but I don't agree with the sentiments, personally. It is entitled *'Death Is Nothing at All'* by Henry Scott-Holland. Yes, it is! It is one of the greatest emotional upsets one can have in life. Whilst it expresses the Christian belief of another life in heaven, to have this read at a funeral at the height of grief is of not much comfort, I think. The poem, *'Footsteps in the Sand'* is far more appropriate and is often read by ministers.

I could include several hymns here. Possibly *'The Lord's My Shepherd,'* *'Abide with Me,'* and *'Jerusalem,'* which I came to know by heart. However, the one hymn which I particularly enjoyed was *'The Day Thou Gavest, Lord, Has Ended.'* Possibly it was because we sang it every week at Bembridge School at the evening service. Each night there was a different vesper, and this one was always sung at the Sunday evening service. It expresses the feeling of the end of the day and, for the deceased, the end of their life:

The day Thou gavest, Lord, is ended

The darkness falls at Thy request

For Thee our morning hymns ascended,

Thy praise shall sanctify our rest.

We thank Thee that Thy Church unsleeping,

While earth rolls onward into light,

Through all the world her watch is keeping,

And rests not now by day or night.

As o'er each continent and island

The dawn leads on another day,

The voice of prayer is never silent,

Nor dies the strain of praise away

The sun that bids us rest in waking

Our brethren 'neath the western sky,

And hour by hour fresh lips are making

Thy wondrous doings heard on high.

So be it, Lord, Thy Throne shall never,

Like earth's proud empires, pass away;

Thy Kingdom stands, and grow for ever,

Till all Thy creatures own Thy sway.

The second hymn, also with remembrances of evening service at school, is 'Saviour, again to Thy dear Name we raise.' Rarely sung at funerals but the sentiments are very real at such a time:

Saviour, again to Thy dear name we raise

With one accord our parting hymn of praise;

We stand to bless Thee ere our worship cease:

Then, lowly kneeling, wait Thy word of peace.

Grant us Thy peace, lord, upon our homeward way;

With Thee began, with Thee shall end the day;

Guard Thou the lips from sin, the hearts from shame,

That in this house have called upon Thy Name.

Grant us Thy peace, Lord, through the coming night;

Turn Thou for us it's darkness into light;

From harm and danger keep Thy people free,

For dark and light are both alike to Thee.

Grant us Thy peace throughout our earthly life,

Our balm in sorrow, and our stray in strife;

Then, when Thy voice shall bid our conflict cease,

Call us, O Lord, to Thine eternal peace.

And lastly, the final line *in 'God be in my Head'* is poignant because it speaks of God being "at my end," evoking a deep sense of comfort and presence in life's final moments.

God be in my head,
And in my understanding;
God be in mine eyes,
And in my looking;
God be in my mouth,
And in my speaking;

God be in my heart,
And in my thinking;
God be at mine end,
And at my departing.

9 780952 619734